Towards
A Shining Life

Aloysius Aseervatham

Copyright © 2022 Aloysius Aseervatham

No part of this book may be used or reproduced by any means, graphic, electronic, or mechanical, including photocopying, recording, taping, or by any information storage retrieval system without the written permission of the copyright owner except in the case of quotations and prayers.

Proisle Publishing Service
1177 Avenue of the Americas, 5th Floor, New York, NY 10036, USA
info@proislepublishing.com

Because of the dynamic nature of the Internet, any web addresses or links contained in this book may have changed since publication and may no longer be valid. The views expressed in this work are solely those of the author and do not necessarily reflect the views of the publisher, and the publisher hereby disclaims any responsibility for them.

ISBN: 978-1-959449-91-1

PROISLE PUBLISHING

TABLE OF CONTENTS

Preface 5

Introduction 7

Acknowledgement... 9

Dedication..9

A Peek at Catholicism...................................... 10

Catholic Prayers and Practices 32

Some Life-Giving Words from the Bible......... 74

Proclaiming the Good News............................. 92

Mary and The Saints.. 101

A Glimpse into the Holy Land........................ 118

The Catholic Church of the Future.................. 157

PREFACE

More than half of the population of the world believes that Jesus Christ is the son of Almighty God and saviour of the world, that He is an ever-present help if they seek Him and live by His teachings. The Christians (followers of Christ) firmly believe that He came to Earth and saved humankind through His death and resurrection. Jesus gave himself sacrificially, so that humankind can receive salvation.

Though Jesus' death and resurrection may not seem possible to non-believers, Christians recognise and firmly believe in the power of God.

It is a pity that many Christian adults have little or no knowledge of Jesus these days owing to the fact that parents and school curriculums neglect to provide a proper religious instruction and motivation to them when they are young.

People seem to fall into two groups – those whose eyes are opened by faith to understand Jesus and those who remain "blind". People who trust in Jesus do so with all their heart and avoid relying on their own insight. Christian faith is the surrender of one's mind, heart and will to say to Jesus, "Let Your Will be done".

The world is in need of a re-energised faith and trust in Jesus and his teachings. Without this, the world will face more chaos and calamity. The most important person who ever walked on the face of this earth is Jesus. His birth is so important that it has split history into two parts and serves as the basis for the calendar most of us use to this day. History tells us that Jesus was a first-century Jew who lived in Israel during the reign of Tiberius Caesar. No one of serious academic achievement would truly deny that Jesus lived.

Our life is meant to shine and glow, not go dim! Praying and repenting for sins is the sure way by which the world can achieve this. We are supposed to repent for our transgressions by turning to Jesus (our Lord and Saviour) and asking for forgiveness.

No one has ever seen Jesus in person except those who lived close to him during his time on Earth. Jesus cannot be seen; However, if people love one another, He will live with them and also in them.

AA   December 2022

INTRODUCTION

God has no beginning or end. He existed before the universe or anything else existed! He is all-knowing, all-powerful, and supremely good.

Unless people understand God's character, they cannot have an intimate relationship with Him.

Christians believe that Jesus was sent by God the Father in heaven to teach people on earth how to live a virtuous life and hence, redeem them from their sinful existence. Jesus had to sacrifice His life to achieve this end.

The revered and sacred writings of any faith is called the scripture. Christian scripture is contained in a book called the Holy Bible which comprises the Old Testament and the New Testament. The Old Testament is foundational in nature, establishing the key principles of Christianity. The New Testament builds on that foundation with further revelation from God. The Four Gospels, or the Good News, written by the disciples of Jesus, known as the four evangelists, namely Matthew, Mark, Luke, and John are part of the New Testament. (Matthew and John were also Apostles of Jesus).

The Old Testament contains many prophecies that are fulfilled in the New. The Old Testament provides the history of the people of Israel, and the New Testament focuses on Jesus' life. The Old Testament shows the wrath of God against transgression/sin (with glimpses of His grace) and the New Testament shows the grace of God towards sinners (with glimpses of His wrath).

It is worth spending some time to find out how the Catholic Church defines and applies the Christian faith via the Bible, Mass, Sacraments etc. and realise why people feel great about being a Catholic.

We live in a world where people are looking for hope. Unfortunately, much of what they hope for is unrealistic and some believe that hope is already lost. The Bible repeatedly assures us that we can find and hold on to a real and living hope. The Catholic church was formed by Jesus with a mission to teach us about love, hope and faith.

The intention of this book is to explain Catholicism and the teachings of the Catholic church, in a nutshell, to those wishing to know the essence of this faith. It is hoped that after reading this book, the reader will be motivated to access some of the excellent books and other resources on Catholicism by Theologians and other leading religious scholars to get a better understanding. In this era of advanced technology, there are many articles and commentaries readily available via social media and other platforms on this subject.

No one is ever hurt by maintaining a teachable spirit. As **Proverbs 1:5** in the Bible states, Let the wise listen and add to their learning, and let the discerning get guidance.

ACKNOWLEDGEMENT

I am extremely thankful to my son Dr. Raj Aseervatham of Brisbane for his eloquent and clear Chapter 6 write up on Holy Land. Many thanks to my friend and Co-author of my book "**Jaffna**" Anton Rajinthrakumar of Canada for his valuable help in reviewing a number of chapters of this book and making suggestions for improvement. I express my sincere gratitude to Mrs. Lynn Thomas, a fellow Parishioner of the Twelve Apostles Catholic Church in Jindalee, Brisbane, for reading the entire manuscript and devoting several hours to refining this book.

Last but not least, I sincerely thank my granddaughter Ms. Zuleikha Aseervatham for tirelessly helping me for many months by formatting the book so efficiently as she has done with six of my other books.

DEDICATION

I dedicate this book to my beloved mother, Rosammah Aseervatham, who strongly instilled in me, her only son, the Catholic Faith of which I am so very proud.

AA

CHAPTER 1
A PEEK AT CATHOLICISM

Catholicism refers to the traditions and beliefs of the Catholic Church; the word Catholic has the meaning "universal". The traditions and beliefs of the Catholic Church refer to her theology, liturgical praying, morals, and spirituality.

Theology is a systematic study of the nature of the divine dogmas (or doctrines) and how different people and cultures express it.

Liturgical praying refers to the engagement in praise, adoration, thanksgiving, petition, and intercession as a community.

Morals are lessons that can be derived from stories or experiences.

Spirituality involves the recognition of a feeling or sense or belief that there is something greater than oneself.

The Catholic Church, also known as the Roman Catholic Church, has about 1.36 billion Catholics worldwide.

THE HIERARCHY OF THE CATHOLIC CHURCH

The Roman Catholic Church was founded by Jesus with the Apostle Peter as the head of the Church. Over many centuries, the Church developed a complex theology and organisational structure led by Peter's successors.

In order to be a true Catholic, it is important to have a sound knowledge of the Teachings of the Catholic Church and how they are expressed through various rituals and lived out in society.

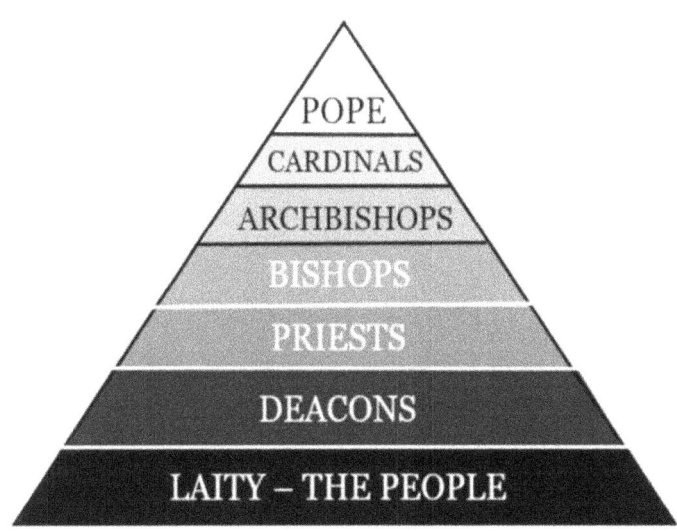

1. Pope

The Pope lives in Vatican City in Rome.

The Pope leads the Catholic Church like a king and is the head of state for the Vatican City.

The Pope's governance of the Catholic Church is termed his papacy. The pope is called by many names, including Papa, Vicar of Christ, Holy Father, and Bishop of Rome.

The Pope has the highest position in the Clergy and is elected by Cardinals under the age of 80. The Pope holds his position until his resignation or death.

The Pope is assisted by Cardinals in the day-to-day exercise of his primatial jurisdiction over the Roman Catholic Church.

The Pope is considered infallible by Catholics as God would not allow his followers to be misled by incorrect decisions.

The Pope receives his authority through an unbroken line of succession that began with Saint Peter. Each Pope receives the 'keys' of Saint Peter and thereby directly carries on the work of Jesus Christ.

2. Cardinal

A cardinal is a leading Bishop (Refer No.4) over all Archbishops (Refer No. 3). Cardinals primarily work as counsellors to the Pope, and many are leaders of dioceses in their home countries. His most important duty is participating in the Papal Conclave, where the new Pope is appointed through election. In addition, he aids in the governing of the Roman Catholic Church.

3. Archbishop

The Archbishop is a Bishop who presides over other Bishops in a district. Other Bishops report to him when in need of assistance or guidance. The Archbishop could be considered a manager of other Bishops within their district.

4. Bishop

Bishops are ministers who hold the full sacrament of Holy Orders. Bishops must be at least 35 years old and must hold a doctorate in theology. This is because Bishops are expected to be experts in canon law (a set of ordinances and regulations) and sacred scripture. The Bishops govern over their local district.

Achieving the title of Bishop by a member of the clergy is important as it is a pre-requisite to all senior rankings thereafter.

5. Priest

To become a Priest, one must participate in the Rite of Ordination ceremony. During this ceremony, they promise to uphold the duties of priesthood and obey all superiors.

There are two categories of priests within the Catholic Church; Diocesan Priests and Religious Order Priests.

Diocesan priests normally serve within the boundaries of their diocese (district) under the authority of their Bishop. Many of these priests are missionary oblates of Mary Immaculate congregation.

A territorial entity constituting a division within a diocese is called a Parish. Each Parish usually has its own church building. A parish is under the pastoral care and clerical jurisdiction of a priest, often termed a parish priest, who might be assisted by one or more priests operating from the parish.

Religious Order Priests, however, vow themselves to a religious order, such as the Jesuits. They wear religious garb and take additional vows of poverty and obedience. Priests are unable to hold personal possessions and they own very little other than their clothes. They typically live in a group house alongside other members of the order. They are not provided with a salary and must follow the orders of their-superior. They live a life of prayer as well as do a lot of retreat work in parishes, schools and retreat venues.

Well Known Catholic Religious Orders are:
- Franciscans (Order of Friars Minor)
- Carthusians (Carthusian Order)
- Jesuits (Society of Jesus)
- Benedictines (Order of St. Benedict)
- Salesians (The Society of St. Francis de Sales)
- Missionaries of Charity.
- Dominicans (Order of Preachers)
- Augustinians (Order of St. Augustine)

6. Deacon

Deacons within the Catholic Church (also referred to as seminarians) are students of the Catholic Church. They are generally in their last phase of training for priesthood. They maintain this role for twelve months. Deacons can practice in many similar ways to priests including witness marriages and perform funerals. However, they cannot say mass nor administer the sacraments.

7. Acolyte

An acolyte is an assistant or follower assisting the celebrant in a religious service or procession. They assist the deacon and priest in liturgical celebrations, especially the eucharistic liturgy.

8. Laity – The people.

Catholic laity are the ordinary members of the Catholic Church who are neither clergy nor recipients of Holy Orders nor vowed to life in a religious order or congregation. Their mission is to follow the word of God and live it out in their lives.

MONKS AND NUNS

Monks and Nuns in the Catholic Church are consecrated religious people who take sacred vows of poverty, chastity, and obedience. Monks and Nuns are also referred to as Reverend Brothers and Reverend Sisters, respectively.

Monks live in Monasteries and Nuns live in Convents.

The Monks and Nuns take a vow of poverty and so they don't own their own car, have no personal bank accounts, and spend as much time as possible in work and in prayer.

There are various religious orders, communities, and congregations. The spirituality of the group is based on the Founder of its congregation, for example Mother Teresa founded the Missionaries of Charity whose members vow to serve "the poorest of the poor." Some communities specialize in teaching and others in hospital work. Some engage in several active missions, and a few devote themselves to a cloistered life of contemplative prayer.

Catholic missionaries — clergy, religious and laypeople — are still active all over the world. Missionary priests oversee rural parishes and bring the Eucharist to remote villages. Lay missionaries teach catechism classes and provide medical care. Religious Sisters run Catholic Schools where they teach and perform the works of mercy. These are just a few snapshots of what today's missionaries do.

THE HOLY BIBLE

The Holy Bible is a collection of religious texts or scriptures sacred in Christianity. It is an anthology—a compilation of texts of a variety of forms—originally written in Hebrew, Aramaic, and Greek.

The Catholic Bible consists of 73 books. The books were written by various people inspired by God, over a period of more than 1,000 years, between 1200 B.C.E. and the first century C.E. (B.C.E means Before Common Era, and C.E means Common Era).

The Bible, containing the word of God, consists of two parts. The first part, **the Old Testament** is a covenant between God and Israel constituting the basis of the Hebrew religion. It has several books by various authors and the books are grouped into 5 sections.

The Bible inspires the catholic doctrine, prayers, and their way of life. The Catholics believe that the Catholic Church continues to be guided by the Holy Spirit through the teaching authority of the Church which addresses the issues of our time and speaks the Truth in one voice. The Catechism of the Catholic Church contains her sacred teachings.

The 5 sections of the Old Testament are:

Genesis, Exodus, Leviticus, Numbers and Deuteronomy

Section 1: Law

Genesis – The book of beginnings.
Exodus – How God delivered the Israelites and made them His special people.
Leviticus – Laws about worship in general and customs & ceremonies.
Numbers – The culmination of the story of Israel's exodus from oppression in Egypt and their journey to take possession of the land God promised their fathers.
Deuteronomy – Moses' restated God's commands originally given to the Israelites some forty years earlier in Exodus and Leviticus.

Moses wrote the above first five books of the Bible
To the Jews, these five books were known collectively as **The Torah.**

Section 2: History

The history of the Israelites is in the following **16 books:**

1. Joshua
2. Judges
3. Ruth
4. 1 Samuel
5. 2 Samuel
6. 1 Kings
7. 2 Kings
8. 1 Chronicles
9. 2 Chronicles
10. Ezra
11. Nehemiah
12. Tobit
13. Judith
14. Esther
15. 1 Maccabees
16. 2 Maccabees

Section 3: The Poetic Books

The Poetic Books deal with good and evil in the world.

The Book of Job discusses why God allows pain.
The Book of Psalms contain the praise songs written by King David.
The Book of Proverbs are short sayings of God's wisdom.
The Book of Ecclesiastes deal with the purpose and value of human life.
Song of Songs or Song of Solomon shows the love of Jesus to His bride, the Church.
The Book of Wisdom urges rulers of the earth to love righteousness and seek wisdom.
The Book of Sirach or Ecclesiasticus addresses issues related to human life and expresses true principles of how to live in the light of God.

The **coming of Jesus** as deliverer and Saviour was prophesied throughout the Old Testament. The Bible is the basis of Abrahamic religions which are Judaism, Christianity and Islam.

Section 4: The Major Prophets

The term "prophet" describes those who deliver messages and teachings from God and warns of the consequences of turning away from Him.

The five major prophets were ***Isaiah, Jeremiah, Lamentations, Ezekiel, and Daniel.***

Section 5: The Minor Prophets

The following were minor prophets.

1. Hosea
2. Joel
3. Amos
4. Obadiah
5. Jonah
6. Micah
7. Nahum
8. Habakkuk
9. Zephaniah
10. Haggai
11. Zechariah
12. Malachi
13. Baruch

The second part of the Bible is the New Testament. It consists of the following:

The **Gospels** or the Good News referring to any message or teaching of Christ.

(The four gospels differ in their emphasis. There are also both similarities and differences. Refer to Chapter 3 for details.)

The **Epistles,** which are the Twenty-one letters, written by various authors, and consists of Christian doctrine, counsel, instruction, and conflict resolution.

Apocalypse (the Book of Revelation), which contains prophetical symbology about the end times.

27 Books of the New Testament:

1. Matthew
2. Mark
3. Luke
4. John
5. Acts of the Apostles
6. Romans
7. 1 Corinthians
8. 2 Corinthians
9. Galatians
10. Ephesians
11. Philippians
12. Colossians
13. 1 Thessalonians
14. 2 Thessalonians
15. 1 Timothy
16. 2 Timothy
17. Titus
18. Philemon
19. Hebrews
20. James
21. 1 Peter
22. 2 Peter
23. 1 John
24. 2 John
25. 3 John
26. Jude
27. Revelation

Christians believe that God had one plan for salvation that was revealed first to the Israelites and then to all peoples through Jesus Christ. The New Testament and Old Testament, then, tell one ongoing story of salvation.

OLD TESTAMENT CHARACTERS

Adam & Eve, the first man and woman created by God introduced human evil into the world when they ate the fruit of a tree God had forbidden them to touch.

Abraham was the Patriarch of the Hebrew Religion. He was also called the Father of All Nations. Christianity began as a movement within Judaism which was the religion of Semitic-speaking Israelites, also known as Hebrews.

Isaac was Abraham's son and the second Patriarch.

Jacob is the third patriarch of the Israelite people and the father of the twelve sons who form the tribes of Israel. He was the grandson of Abraham.

Moses was born to a Hebrew mother and was the most important prophet in Judaism. He was the only man ever to see God 'face to face'. He mediated between God and the people, transforming his people, the Israelites into a nation founded on religious laws. He received the Ten Commandments from God.

David was the king of Israel who founded Jerusalem.

Joseph is Jacob's son and the head official for the Pharaoh (King) of Egypt. Despite being sold into slavery by his brothers, he rose to power in Egypt and saved his family from famine.

Saul (Sha'ul) was the first king of Israel.

David was the second king of Israel.

Absalom was David's son, who attempted to overthrow his father's throne.

Joab was King David's loyal military commander.

Solomon was David's son and the third king of Israel.

Elijah and his successor, **Elisha** were the last great spiritual heroes after the division of Israel into two kingdoms (Israel and Judah).

Noah is a prophet who was instructed by God to build an ark before the world-engulfing flood that occurred a year after the Israelites' exodus from Egypt.

Samson was one of Israel's judges and an epic hero who thwarts the neighbouring Philistines (Canaan) with his superhuman strength.

Rehoboam and **Jeroboam** were the opposing kings who divided Israel into the northern kingdom of Israel and the southern kingdom of Judah.

Ahab and **Jezebel** were the most wicked rulers of Israel.

Esther was a timid Jewish girl who became the queen of Persia (Iran) and stopped the genocide of her people.

Job was the subject of God and Satan's cosmic experiment to measure human faithfulness to God during immense pain.

NEW TESTAMENT CHARACTERS

Jesus (or Jesus Christ), the Son of God, born of the virgin Mary who was crucified for the sins of humanity before resurrecting from the dead.

Mary, a first century Jewish who was conceived by the Holy Spirit to give birth to Jesus.

Peter was one of the Twelve Apostles of Jesus Christ, and one of the first leaders of the early Church and the first Pope.

Mary Magdalene (Mary of Magdala) was one of the Twelve Apostles of Jesus Christ, one of the first leaders of the early Church and one of Jesus' most celebrated disciples. She was famous for being the first person to see the resurrected Christ.

Herod the Great ruled Judea from 37 BC. He initiated a murder of all the infants in Bethlehem to get rid of the baby Jesus.

Pontius Pilate was the fifth governor of the Roman province of Judaea, serving under Emperor Tiberius. He is best known for being the official who presided over the trial of Jesus and ultimately ordered his crucifixion.

John the Apostle or Saint John the Beloved was one of the Twelve Apostles of Jesus. He was one of the Gospel writers.

PAUL, THE APOSTLE

Paul, born as Saul of Tarsus, was a follower of Jesus Christ after he was famously converted to Christianity on the road to Damascus.

Paul's parents were Pharisees—fervent Jewish nationalists who adhered strictly to the Law of Moses and sought to protect their children from "contamination" from the Gentiles. Gentile is a word that usually means "someone who is not a Jew".

While on his way to Damascus to confront the Christians there, Paul is overcome by a flash of heavenly light. He heard the voice of the Lord crying out to him – "Saul, why do you persecute me?" Paul was blinded for three days by this encounter with Jesus and had to be led by hand to Damascus where Ananias of Damascus laid his hands on him and said, "receive thy sight, and be filled with the Holy Spirit". Paul gained his sight back and went to be baptised.

Paul was given the opportunity to do extraordinary things for the kingdom of God.

Paul had decided to preach to gentiles apparently out of his own revelatory experience that this was the mission that had been given him by God when He called him to function as a prophet for this new Jesus movement.

Paul was in prison several times during his ministry, and, almost everywhere he went, there were people who wanted him in prison.

Paul's Epistles

Letters of Paul or Paul's Epistles are the books of the New Testament attributed to him. The letters included affirmations, admonishments, and guidance for various church clergy.

Paul's epistles (letters) to churches include:

- Romans - Paul explains how the gospel works and how to respond.
- 1 Corinthians - Paul admonishes the local church that he had founded in Corinth.
- 2 Corinthians - the Corinthian church resolves their conflict with Paul. Second Corinthians is Paul's a letter of forgiveness and reconciliation.
- Galatians - Paul writes the Galatians an aggressive letter to set them straight on their freedom in Christ.
- Ephesians - Paul outlines doctrines of grace, peace, and salvation, and then instructs the church to walk in a manner worthy of Jesus Christ.
- Philippians - While suffering in prison, Paul finds joy in Christ. He writes to the church at Philippi urging them to take on a Christlike attitude.
- Colossians - This letter explains to the church at Colossae who they are in Christ.
- 1 Thessalonians - The church of Thessalonica is setting a great example for other churches, even though they're being persecuted for their faith. Paul encourages them to "excel still more."
- 2 Thessalonians - The affliction just won't let up on the Thessalonian church, so Paul coaches them on standing firm until Jesus' return.

Disciple Vs. Apostle

Anyone who believes Jesus to be their Lord and Saviour is His Disciple. A person specifically chosen by Jesus to spread the gospel is called an Apostle.

The twelve apostles Jesus had while He was on earth are:

Simon (whom he named Peter), his brother Andrew, James, John, Philip, Bartholomew, Matthew, Thomas, James, (son of Alphaeus), Simon (also called the Zealot), Judas son of James, and Judas Iscariot. Once Jesus had ascended into heaven, the apostles gathered to choose Matthias as a replacement for Judas Iscariot who after betraying Jesus hung himself.

Reading the Bible

One can find direction for their life and learn how to best serve the Lord who gave His life for them by reading the Bible consistently.

There is no set method to read the Bible. It is up to the person to decide where to begin. It is sensible to start at the beginning (Genesis), but some prefer to start with the New Testament.

Whatever method chosen, always pray to God before starting to read a Bible passage to reveal Himself and speak through His Word. When reading the Bible, ask "what does the passage I read teach me about God, and how can I apply it to my life?"

Always approach the Bible with the intention of understanding the big picture.

It is not always easy to understand the Bible passages.

Learn to gather and absorb the situation, actions, and ideas being conveyed by the letters and words.

Bear in mind that the Bible was translated from multiple languages (Hebrew, Greek, Aramaic etc.) into English, therefore, there may be translation errors!

Reading and understanding the Bible verses by people is a personal religious or spiritual practice. Many churches encourage people to read and discuss Bible collectively. This is called Bible Study.

The purpose of Bible study is to grasp the true meaning of Bible verses through discussion!

When interpreting a Bible Verse, it is important to remember the context in which certain word or words are used in it.

It is easy to misinterpret a figurative language for literal language. For example, when Jesus says "**I am the gate**" he is not saying that he is a physical gate!

Another example is when Jesus says, "It is difficult for a rich man to enter heaven than a camel to go through the eye of a needle". Here, the eye of the needle refers to a **gate** which is so small compared to the size of the camel and it must get down on its knees to go through! Thus, knowing the context will often help us understand what is truly meant.

When commencing to read the Bible one must be in the right frame of mind and pray to God asking for wisdom and understanding.
It is also difficult for the mind to be alert when one's stomach is full, or the brain is tired!

It is a show of disrespect for God if one skims over the material that they don't understand. Be ever ready to do some research. Ensure that the Bible is read with proper understanding.

Where is it in the Bible?

The Bible may need to be read as a whole book to find the answer to a particular question, any part of which can be twisted or misinterpreted!

THE SIX COMMANDMENTS OF THE CATHOLIC CHURCH

i. Attend Mass on Sundays and Holydays of Obligation.
ii. Fast and abstain on the days of obligation.
iii. Confess at least once a year.
iv. Receive the Holy Eucharist during Easter time.
v. Contribute to the support of Parishes.
vi. Do not marry without the Bishop's permission, persons who are not Catholics, or who are related within three degrees of kindred; nor privately marry without witnesses; Don't solemnize marriage at forbidden times.

Living like Jesus

Jesus taught the Golden Rule during His Sermon on the Mount: He said, treat others the way you want to be treated. As you do so, you will strengthen your relationships and be happier.

The life of a Catholic should include love, joy, peace, patience, kindness, goodness, generosity, gentleness, faithfulness, modesty, self-control, and chastity.

The Holy Sacraments

In order that we might easily understand the hidden power of God through the redemption carried out by Jesus Christ, He ordained that His power should be manifested to us through the intervention of sensible signs; called the Sacraments.

The Catholic Church teaches that Christ instituted Sacraments, which Catholics will take part in at different stages of their lives.

The 7 Sacraments are:
(Refer to Chapter 2 for details)

1. Baptism
2. Confirmation
3. Penance (reconciliation or confession)
4. Eucharist
5. Matrimony
6. Holy Orders
7. Anointing of the Sick

When receiving a sacrament, Catholics are touched by Jesus. They become what they receive and are strengthened for life's journey.

CHAPTER 2

CATHOLIC PRAYERS AND PRACTICES

The formative years of individuals are typically the early childhood years of their life. It is during this period that an individual's brain and nervous system develop the fastest. What happens in their life during these years can affect their physical and mental development and hence, the extent of success in their lives. The events in the life of a person during this time leave a lasting imprint on his or her brain, consequently affecting the development of their personality and skills.

Over the next several years, various cognitive functions, including decision making, information retention, and emotion management will also develop.

Children with healthy childhood experiences will reap the most benefits during their adult lives.

Children who have experienced emotional neglect, physical abuse, and socioeconomic stress, can still thrive in life. However, these early misfortunes can cause lasting self-destructive behavioural and emotional issues as they grow.

Healthy social and emotional development also occurs during the formative years. During these years, the child learns what love and care are. They learn how to socialize with others and can identify what behaviours are acceptable.

An ideal parent would possess good physical and mental health, especially during their child's formative years. A child needs at least one stable parent or guardian to guide them through their life. It is then and only then, that a child can develop strength and resilience.

Children develop both physically and mentally at different paces during the formative years. Therefore, consulting with a paediatrician, if possible, can allow parents to address any concerns about their child's development at an early stage.

Religious faith also has a significant role in a child's physical and mental development. Most children are raised in their parents' religious beliefs. Religious beliefs are also imparted in schools through their religious programs.

If a person was born in an orthodox Catholic family, he or she would be admitted into a Catholic school. First, they would be introduced to some simple prayers which had to be memorised. The teacher would normally be a lay person but occasionally a priest or a teacher of catholic principles (catechist) would give instructions.

As an introduction, the concept of one God in the Catholic faith and the Trinity which means three persons in the one God, namely, the Father, the Son and the Holy Spirit would be taught. Additionally, the details of the Birth of Jesus would be explained, and some Catholic practices introduced.

As part of the instructions, some traditional prayers recited during **Holy Mass**, which is central to the Catholic faith would be given importance. During the Holy Mass Catholics spend time together with God to receive His graces and blessings.

Through the priest, Catholics offer Jesus' Body and Blood, just as Jesus offered Himself to God the Father on the Cross and at the Last Supper.

The 'formless' God

God is viewed by the believers as a Supreme Being in the Catholic Faith. God is described without reference to gender, the reason being that God is formless.

Holy Trinity Further Explained

The mystery of the Holy Trinity as we already know, the central mystery of the Catholic faith and life. God reveals himself as Father, Son, and Holy Spirit. The doctrine of the Trinity includes three truths of faith, the Trinity is One. The Catholics do not speak of three gods but of one God with a unity of Persons in one divine nature. Second, the Divine Persons are distinct from each other. Father, Son, and the Holy Spirit are not three appearances or modes of God, but three identifiable persons, each fully God in a way distinct from the others. Third, the Divine Persons are in relation to each other.

Jesus was sent by God the father to His chosen people to give them the fulness of life by the ultimate expression of His love when He sacrificed Himself to redeem them from sin.

The Advocate

Jesus said to his apostles before he left them after his resurrection that his father will send an advocate in his name. The Holy Spirit who will teach them everything and remind all that he had said to them. God, the Father speaks to people through the Holy Spirit.

Amid troubles we can sense the presence of Holy Spirit. The Holy Spirit lives within us. The fruit of the Spirit is **love, joy, peace, patience, kindness, goodness, faithfulness, gentleness, and self-control.**

By the death and resurrection of Jesus people are given a new nature. They also received **grace** from the Holy Spirit which is the ability to do what they couldn't do by themselves before. Sin ruled them before and now they can overcome it.

Sign of the Cross

The sign of the cross is used throughout Christian liturgies, in moments of need or danger, at the beginning and end of a prayer, and on numerous other occasions.

The "sign of the cross" made by saying the words below while touching one's right hand to the forehead first (Father) then to the lower chest (Son), then to the left shoulder and the right shoulder (Holy Spirit) and finally with both hands clasped together saying the word **Amen**.

The words said are:

In the name of the Father, Son, and the Holy Spirit Amen.

Common Catholic Prayers said during Mass

The Confiteor (or 'I confess')

This is a prayer that is said during the beginning of the Holy Mass in the Catholic Church.

I confess to almighty God
and to you, my brothers and sisters,
that I have greatly sinned,
in my thoughts and in my words,
in what I have done and in what I have failed to do,
through my fault, thorough my fault,
through my most grievous fault;
therefore I ask blessed Mary ever-Virgin,
all the Angels and Saints,
and you, my brothers and sisters,
to pray for me to the Lord our God,

Lord's Prayer (or 'The Our Father')

This is a prayer taught by Jesus to his apostles and is recited during Mass,

Our Father,

who art in heaven,

hallowed be thy name;

thy kingdom come;

thy will be done on earth as it is in heaven.

Give us this day our daily bread;

and forgive us our trespasses

as we forgive those who trespass against us;

and do not let us fall into temptation

but deliver us from evil.

Amen

The "Gloria"

During the introductory part of the Holy Mass, Catholics say (or sing) the Gloria. Gloria is a Latin word meaning "glory" and is recited to give glory to God.

Glory to God in the highest,
and on earth peace to people of good will.
We praise you; we bless you,
we adore you; we glorify you.
We give you thanks for your great glory,

Lord God, heavenly King,
O God, almighty Father.
Lord Jesus Christ, only Begotten Son,
Lord God, Lamb of God, Son of the Father,
You take away the sins of the world
 have mercy on us.
You take away the sins of the world,
 receive our prayer.
You are seated at the right hand of the Father:
have mercy on us.
For you alone are the Holy One,
You alone are the Lord,
You alone are the Most High, Jesus Christ,
With the Holy Spirit, in the glory of God the Father.
Amen.

Profession of Catholic Faith

When a person is accepted into the Catholic Church, they are required to recite the core beliefs of the Catholic faith. This recitation is called the Profession of Catholic Faith. There are two versions of the profession, known as the **'Apostles' Creed'** and the **'Nicene Creed'**: 'Creed' meaning a formal statement of Catholic beliefs.

The Apostles' Creed was written by the Apostles of Jesus themselves, while the Nicene Creed was developed at a Church Council.

The Nicene Creed expresses the Apostles' Creed more clearly to preserve, guard and pass on the Catholic faith to future generations.

Nicene Creed

We believe *in God, the Father, the Almighty, maker of heaven and earth and all that is seen and unseen.*

We believe *in one Lord, Jesus Christ, the only Son of God, eternally begotten of the Father, God from God, Light from Light, true God from true God, begotten, not made, one in Being with the Father. Through him all things were made.*

For us men and for our salvation he came down from heaven: and by the Holy Spirit was incarnated; he was born of the Virgin Mary and became man. For our sake he was crucified under Pontius Pilate; he suffered, died, and was buried. On the third day he rose again in fulfilment of the Scriptures; he ascended into heaven and is seated at the right hand of the Father. He will come again in glory to judge the living and the dead, and His kingdom will have no end.

We believe *in the Holy Spirit, the Lord, the giver of life, who proceeds from the Father and the Son. With the Father and the Son, he is worshipped and glorified. He has spoken through the Prophets.*

We believe *in one holy catholic and apostolic Church. We acknowledge one baptism for the forgiveness of sins. We look for the resurrection of the dead, and the* *life of the world to come.*

Amen.

Sample Morning, Night and Mealtime Prayers

A Morning Prayer on waking up

Dear Lord, I thank you for giving me a new day. Forgive my errors of yesterday and bless me to walk closer in Your way today. Please help me to begin my day today with confidence; shine through me so that every person I meet today may feel Your presence in me. Be my guide throughout the day. Amen.

A Night Prayer on retiring to bed

Grant me a good night's sleep God. Help me to wake up in the morning, with a joyful smile. Thank you, Lord, for your protection and your presence to guide me today. Good night, Lord.

A prayer before a meal

O Lord! bless me and these gifts, which I am about to receive from Thy bounty. Amen.

THE HOLY MASS

The introductory rite of the Holy Mass allows a moment of reflection as Catholics are invited to confess and repent their sins. This is done by reciting the Confiteor.

Following Confiteor, passages from both the Old and New Testament are read. The central focus of the Old Testament is God's Law for a holy standard of living. The New Testament maintains these Laws and introduces God's Grace, which opens the door for salvation from our sins. The New Testament readings include passages from the Acts of the Apostles, Revelation to John, and the Epistles or letters written by apostles to various Catholic churches. This section concludes with the priest delivering a sermon (or homily).

The subsequent part of the Holy Mass is called the Eucharist. This is when Catholics give thanks and offer themselves to God. This is symbolised by the bread becoming Jesus' body, and wine becoming Jesus' blood. The Eucharist refers to the real presence of Jesus Christ through the bread and wine. The Catholics receive the Eucharist when they attend the Holy Mass.

To conclude the Holy Mass, the priest says a short prayer and blesses everyone in the name of the Father, the Son and the Holy Spirit. The Congregation leaves the service knowing that they have worshipped God and thereby, are strengthened by Him to continue serving Him in their daily lives.

The prayers recited during Holy Mass include the sign of the cross, the Lord's prayer and the profession of faith.

The Rites Explained

- **Introductory Rites:** As the Priest, cross bearers, candle bearers and ministers enter the church the congregation sings a gathering song (or hymn). This encourages the congregation to stand together and sing, symbolising that they are gathered as a community and as one body.

    The priest kisses the altar to show deep respect and reverence to Jesus. The congregation makes the sign of the cross together with the priest. *By the sign of the cross, the congregation is marked with the name of God; they have clothed themselves with the Holy Spirit.*

    The Priest recites an official greeting – *'may the grace*

and peace of Lord Jesus Christ and the love of God who is our Father, and the Communion of the Holy Spirit be with you'

- **Penitential Rite**: The priest invites the congregation to recall their sins and ask God for forgiveness; they then recite the 'Kyrie Eleison' (meaning *Lord have mercy*). Then, the **'Gloria'** is sung. This hymn was first sung by the angels when Jesus was born in Bethlehem. Following this, the priest says a prayer addressing God the Father through Christ in the Holy Spirit.

- **Liturgy of the word:** To begin, a passage from the Old Testament is read by a member of the congregation. Then, the congregation sings a responsorial song taken from the Book of Psalms written by Solomon, a follower of God. A second passage taken from the New Testament is also read by a member of the congregation.

The priest introduces a related passage from one of the Gospels (of Matthew, Mark, Luke, or John) in the New Testament. Then, the congregation makes the sign of the cross on their forehead, lips, and heart to signify that they believe, speak, and love the words of Christ. *They stand and listen carefully as the Priest reads the Gospel.*

The priest explains all readings in what is called a

homily as the congregation is seated. After a moment of silence, the congregation stands and makes a profession of their faith through the Creed, at the end of which they pray for the pope, the clergy, the church, their deceased relatives, and friends and so on.

- **The Liturgy of the Eucharist:** As the Liturgy of the Eucharist begins, the priest washes his hands. It is a sign of the priest's spiritual cleansing before handling the consecrated Eucharist which is holy and sacred. It is also an act of humility and respect to God. As the priest washes his hands, he recites the words: *'wash me, Oh Lord, of my iniquity, and cleanse me from my sins'.*

- **Eucharistic prayer**: The congregation gives thanks and praise to God. Then, they sing the affirmation of praise *'Holy, Holy, Holy...'.*

The bread and wine are laid on the altar, signifying the preparation for the most important moment of the Mass, which is the changing of the bread and wine, through the power of the Holy Spirit, into the actual body and blood of Jesus Christ. The priest raises the bread and recites the words said by Jesus during His Last Supper with his disciples, *'take this all of you and eat it, for this is my body, which will be given up for you'.* The bread then becomes the actual body of Jesus Christ.

The priest raises the chalice of wine and recites in a similar fashion, *'take this all of you and drink from it, for this is the chalice of my blood, the blood of the new and eternal covenant, which will be poured out for you and for many, for the forgiveness of sins, do this in memory of me'*. The wine becomes the actual blood of Jesus Christ.

Then the congregation sings the Memorial Acclamation: *'We proclaim your death O Lord until you come again'*.

'Through Him and with Him and in Him…AMEN.'

- **Communion Rite**: The congregation says the Lord's Prayer, the 'Our Father'. Then, they offer the sign of peace to each other, saying 'peace be with you'. This act is a reminder for the congregation that to receive or offer peace to others, they must resolve their own personal conflicts.

  The congregation receives the body and blood of Christ in Holy Communion. After communion, they pray that the Eucharist will strengthen their spiritual and daily lives.

- **Concluding Rites:** The congregation stands as the priest says a final prayer. He then blesses the congregation and says, *'mass has ended, go and serve the Lord'*. God does not leave those of the congregation alone in the world, he goes with them as they have received the Eucharist.

The Priest, cross bearers, candle bearers and ministers leave the altar, as the congregation sings a recessional song of praise.

Liturgical Objects Used During the Holy Mass

The Alb – a full-length white garment worn by the priest. It is a symbol that recalls the Priest's baptism.
The Stole – a vestment that the priest wears over Alb and is symbolic of their authority and dedication to service.
Different colour stole is used for different occasion ☐ **Green** is worn during ordinary time ☐ **White** is worn during the feasts of Our Lady and of Our Lord ☐ **Red** is worn during a feast of a martyr (signifies blood of the martyr, or the fire of the holy spirit) ☐ **Purple** or **pink** are worn during Advent (birth of Jesus) and Lent (death and resurrection of Jesus)
The Lectionary – the book of readings.
Roman Missal contains all the prayers.
The linens – **corporal** (placemat) and **purificator** (napkin).

> The two sacred vessels are:
> - The **ciborium** (holds the bread that will become Jesus' body)
> - The **chalice** (holds the wine which will become Jesus' blood)

Transubstantiation

Although the bread and wine do not visually change, they become the actual body and blood of Christ. The **substance changes**, not the appearance.

In order to better understand the mystery of the real presence of Christ in the Eucharist in light of a new philosophy of the nature of reality that is more in line with contemporary physics, the terms **transignification** and **transfinalisation** are used.

Other items used by priest at Mass

Lavabo is a device used by the Priest to wash hands. It consists of an ewer, or pitcher, and a bowl that catches the water as it falls off the Priest's hands. This device is used in preparation before handling the consecrated Eucharist; this is a sign of spiritual cleansing.

Ambo or **Lectern** is where the books of readings are kept and read from.

The **Chasuble** is a garment worn over the Priest's Alb. It is symbolic of the Priest's love for the people. Different colours are worn for different occasions much like the stole. The colours are also green, white, red, purple/pink.

Catholic Devotions

Two popular Catholic devotions are Benediction, and Novenas.

Benediction is the exposition of the eucharistic host in a *Monstrance* and the blessing of the people with it by a priest after the congregation says some prayers and sings hymns of praise.

Monstrance

Some churches have a monstrance with the host perpetually available for prayer and adoration.

The consecrated communion or eucharist is stored in a locked box in the church. This box is called the **tabernacle.** Catholics show reverence and adoration by genuflecting whenever passing in front of the tabernacle.

Novenas

Jesus' disciples and Mary waited together, for the Holy Spirit to guide them after His ascension into heaven. After nine days, the Holy Spirit came down on them. Since then, the novena (or nine day) prayer method became popular.

Novenas in petition ask God to answer a prayer or ask a

saint for their intercession.

The Holy Hour

A Holy Hour is a devotion in which the catholic congregation spends one hour in prayer, dedicating that time to be with Jesus. It is time spent with God, experiencing his loving presence and bringing our prayers and praises before him.

Feasts

The feast of the Resurrection of Jesus, called Pascha (Easter), is the greatest of all holy days and as such it is called the "Feast of Feasts".

The celebrations of greatest importance include all Sundays and Holy Days of Obligation and are called solemnities.

In the Catholic Church, holy days of obligation are days on which the faithful are expected to attend Mass, observe fasting and abstinence and engage in rest from work and recreation.

The Holy days of obligation other than Sundays include:

- Mary the mother of God – January 1
- Assumption of the Blessed Virgin Mary into heaven – August 15
- All Saints Day - November 1
- Immaculate Conception of Mary – December 8
- Christmas – December 25

All Saints, Mary the mother of God (January 1) and the Assumption are not Holy Days of obligation if they fall on a Saturday or Monday.

A holy day of obligation in one country may not necessarily be one in another country!

Retreats

Retreats take a variety of formats, but with all of them an individual or group leave their life behind (as far as possible) for a period of time and try to focus on their relationship with God and with their faith.

The Way of The Cross

The Way of the Cross is a traditional devotion in honour of the trials and death of Jesus. It is also known as **Stations of the Cross**.

The Way of the Cross is a mini pilgrimage through the events that covered the final hours of Jesus' life on earth. In most Catholic Churches there are painted or carved images depicting the Way of the Cross, around the walls of the Church.

Way of the Cross is a series of 14 pictures or carvings of stations portraying events in the Passion of Christ, from his condemnation by Pontius-Pilate to his entombment.

The processional route in the Old City of Jerusalem *is called* **Via Dolorosa**. It is a winding route from the Antonia Fortress to the Church of the Holy Sepulchre — a distance of about 600 metres. It is marked by fourteen Stations of the Cross, nine of which are outside, in the streets, with the remaining five stations being currently inside the Church of the Holy Sepulchre.

The stations are mostly prayed in the Catholic Churches during Lent on Wednesdays and Fridays, and especially on Good Friday.

Lent season begins on **Ash Wednesday,** six and a half weeks before Easter, and provides a 40-day period for fasting and abstinence (Sundays are excluded), in imitation of Jesus Christ's fasting in the wilderness before he began his public ministry.

Everyone of age 14 and up is required to abstain from consuming meat during the lent season. On Ash Wednesday and Good Friday: Everyone of age 18 to 59 must fast, unless exempt due to usually a medical reason.

Ash Wednesday **derives its name from the saying "Remember that you are dust, and unto dust you shall return."** The ashes are prepared by burning palm leaves from the previous year's Palm Sunday celebrations. Palm Sunday is the day Jesus entered into Jerusalem and was greeted by the people waving palm branches. For Christians, it is a reminder of the welcoming of Jesus into their hearts and of their willingness to follow him.

The series of stations and a short prayer

i. <u>Jesus is condemned to death.</u>

Prayer
Jesus, you have done nothing wrong to be put to death. It is I who have done the wrong. Please forgive me.

ii. <u>Jesus is made to carry the cross.</u>

Prayer
By carrying the heavy cross, you have earned pardon for my sins and the sins of the world. Jesus, help me to carry my cross-till death.

iii. <u>Jesus falls the first time.</u>

Prayer
Jesus, the soldiers hit you when you fell to make you get up. O' Lord Jesus, never let me to fall into sin again.

iv. <u>Jesus meets his holy mother.</u>

Prayer
Tears of sadness filled the eyes of Mary, when she saw you Jesus her son in a pitiful condition. Mother of sorrows forgive me.

v. <u>Simon of Cyrene is made to carry the cross.</u>

Prayer
I have hurt you immensely by my sins instead of helping you. O' Jesus, please make me your strong helper as Simon did, from now on.

vi. <u>Veronica wipes Jesus' face.</u>

Prayer
When Veronica wiped your face, Jesus you left your image on her veil. Please never let me to forget this image of your holy face.

vii. <u>Jesus falls the second time.</u>

Prayer
O' Jesus when you fell the second time, the soldiers hit you again. You got up. Please help me to go for confession as soon as I can if I should fall into sin.

viii. <u>The women of Jerusalem weep over Jesus.</u>

Prayer
Some holy women saw you Jesus and wept tears of sorrow. But you said, 'weep for yourselves and for your children.' Please help me also to weep for committing sins that offend you.

ix. <u>Jesus falls the third time.</u>

Prayer
O' Jesus, the cross was heavy, and your body was weakened with pain making you fall again. Jesus, help me to avoid falling into sin repeatedly.

x.   Jesus is stripped of his garments.
Prayer
Your robe was sticking to the wounds O' Jesus and it hurt you terribly when they tore it off. Thank you for bearing the pain to help me stay away from sin.

xi.   Jesus is nailed to the cross.
Prayer
The nails cut through your hands and feet O' Lord when they crucified you. Thank you for your silent suffering that proves your love for me.

xii.   Jesus dies on the cross.
Prayer
Hanging on the cross, you showed your immense mercy by saying "Father, forgive them, for they know not, what they are doing". Please, O' Jesus forgive me for my sins.

xiii. Jesus is taken down from the cross.
Prayer
After three long hours of pain and agony you died, O Jesus. Mary, your beloved mother standing at the foot of the Cross received your holy body and was in great sorrow. Mother of sorrows, pray for us sinners.

xiv.   Jesus' body is placed in the sepulchre.
Prayer
Your body was placed in the sepulchre, o' Jesus. But you rose from the dead on the third day as you promised. In your glorious death and resurrection, I place my complete faith and trust.

Praying the Stations of the Cross is **a traditional way of praying during Lent.** Catholics pray this familiar prayer to be with Jesus Christ, who walked this journey carrying the cross, the instrument of his death, out of love and commitment to them.

Procedures during the Sacraments

i. Baptism

When a child is born, they are admitted within a short time of the birth, into the Catholic community through a sacrament called Baptism. This ceremony celebrates the child's induction into the Catholic faith.

Baptism serves as the gateway to all the other sacraments.

Baptism is sometimes called Christening. It is a rite of admission into the Church through the use of water, just as Jesus Christ was baptized in the River Jordan.

Undergoing baptism, cleanses the person of the original sin of Adam and Eve. Original sin is the Christian doctrine which says that because of the sin of Adam and Eve, original innocence is lost, and all subsequent human beings are born into a state of sinfulness. Baptism brings the person back into a State of Grace.

In a typical Baptism celebration, parents and their chosen godparents bring the child to their priest or minister who then pours water on the child's forehead and say some prayers. During the ceremony the parents and godparents vow to be a good influence on the child. They each hold a lighted candle all throughout the baptismal rites.

A baptismal certificate is signed by the officiating priest and serves as an official document and record of the time and date of baptism, as well as something to keep as a memento for the parents.

Usually, the parents and guests have a party to celebrate the occasion.

ii. Confirmation

Confirmation, is a Christian rite by which admission to the church, established previously in infant baptism, is said to be confirmed, usually before the child receives the Eucharist.

While baptism sets a child on the path to eternal life, confirmation intensifies that beginning and blesses with the gifts of the Holy Spirit.

A bishop leads the people in praying for the Holy Spirit to rest upon those confirmed. He addresses each candidate by name and recites a special confirmation prayer.

The Roman Catholic Church views Confirmation as a sacrament instituted by Jesus Christ. It confers the gifts of the Holy Spirit (wisdom, understanding, knowledge, counsel, fortitude, piety, and fear of the Lord) upon the recipient, who must be a baptized person at least seven years old.

A comprehensive confirmation program is more than just a class. It seeks to provide experiences and opportunities in which the child can be shaped as a Christian.

iii. Penance (Confession or Reconciliation)

Penance is a sacrament in which a member of the Church confesses sins to a priest and is given absolution.

The penitent says the following prayer before going to confession.

O most merciful God! Prostrate at your feet, I implore your forgiveness. I sincerely desire to leave all my evil ways and to confess my sins with all sincerity to you and to your priest. I am a sinner, have mercy on me, O Lord. Give me a lively faith and a firm hope in the Passion of my Redeemer. Give me, for your mercy's sake a sorrow for having offended so good a God. Mary, my mother, refuge of sinners, pray for me that I may make a good confession. Amen.

The following then takes place:

1. The penitent goes to confession either behind a screen or face to face.

2. After the priest greets the penitent in the name of Christ, he makes the sign of the cross. He may then recite a reading from Scripture, after which the penitent says: "Bless me Father for I have sinned. It has been (state how long) since my last confession. These are my sins."

3. The penitent tells the sins simply and honestly to the priest and may tell the circumstances and the root causes of their sins.

4. The penitent listens to the advice the priest give and accepts the penance from him. Then the Act of Contrition for the sins is recited by the penitent.

5. The priest will then dismiss the penitent with the words of praise: "Give thanks to the Lord for He is good. You respond: "For His mercy endures forever." The priest will then conclude with: "The Lord has freed you from your sins. Go in peace." And you respond by saying: "Thanks be to God."

6. The penitent spends some time in prayer with the Lord thanking and praising Him for the gift of His

mercy. (The penitent performs the penance as soon as possible, after reciting the prayer called 'Act of Contrition')

Act of Contrition

Oh my God,
I am sorry for my sins with all my heart.
In choosing to do wrong
And failing to do good,
I have sinned against you
whom I should love above all things.
I firmly intend, with your help,
to do penance,
to sin no more,
and to avoid whatever leads me to sin.
Our Saviour Jesus Christ, suffered and died for us.
In His name, my God, have mercy. Amen.

iv.   Eucharist

The Eucharist also known as **Holy Communion** is central to the Catholic Church. The Catholics go to Sunday service or mass at the church to receive Holy Communion. Jesus is bodily present in the Holy communion which can be received in any daily mass also. The Catholic Church has rules and guidelines about who can receive Holy Communion. First holy communion is usually given to kids around seven years old, although some dioceses have, in recent years, moved that forward a year or two.

In any case, only baptised Catholics are eligible to receive Communion.

v. Anointing of the Sick

The anointing of the sick by a priest is often a Catholic Christian's final sacrament. It is given to people who are in danger of becoming sicker from a serious illness and it is also given to those who are likely to die soon.

The steps involved are:

- Priest, family, and friends gather to pray.
- Priest sprinkles holy water on the sick.
- God's Word is proclaimed.
- Priest lays hands on the sick person's head and anoints with oil on their forehead and hands.

vi. Holy Orders

There are three holy orders:

1. A Deacon - who can preach and distribute Holy Communion (but not transubstantiate it).
2. An ordained Priest - who has the power to change bread and wine into the Body and Blood of Christ (transubstantiation) and to forgive sins.
3. An ordained Bishop – who with the complete fullness of the priesthood, has also the power to confirm and to ordain deacons, priests, and other bishops.

vii. Matrimony

Matrimony (i.e., marriage), is a lasting commitment between a man and a woman to be united in such a way that they become one flesh, each belonging to one another. It is established for the good of each other and for the procreation of children.

Marriage is conferred by a priest, or bishop. The man and woman express their consent to marry, before God and the Church.

The exchange of consent between a man and a woman is an essential part of the marriage-ceremony.

The Catholic Church does not permit divorce for valid sacramental marriages.

In fact, a valid sacramental marriage is impossible to dissolve thereby making divorce not possible if the marriage was sacramental.

Catholic wedding vows are generally preceded by three questions from the priest:

"Have you come here freely and without reservation to give yourselves to each other in marriage?"

"Will you honour each other as man and wife for the rest of your lives?"

"Will you accept children lovingly from God, and bring them up according to the law of Christ and his Church?"

The bride and groom say *"I do"* to the wedding vows.

Preparing for marriage in the Catholic Church

- Contact the parish church of the couple's choice in which marriage would take place.

- Speak to the priest or someone else who coordinates weddings to initiate the process. (do this about one year in advance of the desired wedding date).

- Attend marriage preparation classes.

- Talk about many different aspects that affect a married relationship such as sexual attitudes, the number of children, how to raise children, personal interactions, and more.

- Coordinate the overall logistics of the special day.

THE TEN COMMANDMENTS

The Ten Commandments are a list of religious laws that were divinely revealed to Moses by God and engraved on two stone tablets. Sin means, an offense against a religious or a moral law; an act which severs one from God.

First Commandment

I am the LORD your God: you shall not have strange Gods before me.

Sin(s):
- ☐ Idolatry:
    - o Superstition
    - o Black Magic
    - o Sorcery
    - o Vain observance
    - o Divination

Idolatry is anything that you love, treasure, prioritize, identify with, or look to, for need fulfillment outside of God.

Second Commandment

You shall not take the name of the Lord your God in vain.

Sins:
- ☐ Irreverently using God's name
- ☐ Cursing

Third Commandment

Remember to keep the Lord's Day, holy.

Sin(s):
> Engaging in work or activities that hinder the worship due to God and the joy proper to the Lord's Day.

Legitimate excuses from Sunday obligation would be illness, job obligations and family obligations, i.e., a caregiver for an ill member of the family.

Fourth Commandment

Honour your father and your mother.

Sins:
- ☐ Not loving and respecting parents.
- ☐ Not obeying parents in all that is not sinful.
- ☐ Not giving parents material and moral support in old age, in times of illness, and distress.

Fifth Commandment

You shall not kill.

Sins:
- ☐ Intentional homicide (murder, abortion)
- ☐ Doing anything that with the intention of indirectly causing the death of a person
- ☐ Refusing assistance to a person in danger
- ☐ Formal cooperation in an abortion
- ☐ Exploiting human embryos for disposable biological material
- ☐ Euthanasia
- ☐ Suicide (grave psychological disturbances, anguish, can diminish the responsibility of one committing suicide)
- ☐ Causing scandal / Bad example
- ☐ Kidnapping /hostage taking
- ☐ Fighting, anger, hatred, revenge
- ☐ Drunkenness
- ☐ Reckless driving
- ☐ Claiming the right directly to destroy an innocent human life.

Sixth Commandment

You shall not steal.

Sins:
- ☐ Stealing
- ☐ Cheating
- ☐ Discrimination
- ☐ Refusing or withholding a just wage

Seventh Commandment

You shall not bear false witness against your neighbour.

Sins:
- ☐☐ Lies
- ☐☐ Detraction [Revealing without good reason the hidden faults of others]
- ☐☐ Calumny/Slander: [Injuring the good name of another by lying]

Eighth Commandment

You shall not covet your neighbour's wife.

Sins:
- ☐ Lust ☐
- ☐ Lack of moderation with alcohol ☐
- ☐ Voyeurism ☐

Ninth Commandment

You shall not commit adultery.

Sins:
- ☐ Lust
- ☐ Fornication [sexual relations of the unmarried]
- ☐ Pornography
- ☐ Prostitution
- ☐ Rape / Incest
- ☐ Adultery [marital infidelity]
- ☐ Divorce (Note that an innocent victim of divorce, an abandoned spouse, does not contravene the moral law.)
- ☐ Cohabitation / "trial marriage"

Tenth Commandment

You shall not covet your neighbour's goods.

Sins:
- ☐ Wanting what someone else has

Note:

One of the most easily broken commandments is the first commandment.

Sins explained further

The most annoying problem of man is his alienation from God. His estrangement from God is his own making, out of his own choice.

Every sin is man's turning away from God. Man allows his life to be taken over by the powers of the evil one. The Church reminds us that God is with us to free us from the darkness of sin. Man's bodily paralysis is connected to his sinful state and healing comes about with the redemption from sin.

Mortal or grave sins are to be contrasted with venial or minor sins, which are usually committed with less self-awareness of wrongdoing. A venial sin only weakens the sinner's union with God. it is not a deliberate turning away from Him.

We must remember that what is impossible for man is possible for God.

If we seek His help, God sends His spirit to work in us and bring about supernatural transformation.

Everyone who commits sin is a slave to sin. We need to be watchful against the evil power trying to gain entry and take hold of our life.

Satan lodges within us with the sole purpose of destroying us. When we allow anger, lust, jealousy, and other such negative thoughts we are giving a foothold to Satan.

Irrespective of the extent of the crippling effect of our sins in our lives, Jesus promises us, "If the Son sets you free, you will be free indeed".

God Reveals Himself

God reveals himself to many people. People like Abraham, Moses, Isaac, and other holy people even spoke/speak to God!

God sends his Spirit to save his people. We need to ask him to send his spirit to help us and others in times of need or distress. We should also remember to thank God for his benevolence and help.

We can seek God through prayer, Scripture reading, worship, and fellowship. In seeking God, we come to know Him better and we bring Him glory.

Prayer time

Praying can be done at scheduled times or spontaneously.

The best time to pray is, however, early mornings. The idea here is that we seek God before we meet the fellow humans or before running into the chaos of the world!

Anyone rising early and praying will find favour says the Bible! "Manna' (an edible substance in the form of bread which God provided for the Israelites during their travels in the desert) was available to only those who got up early before it got melted by the fleeting rays of the sun.

Any prayer said in the morning will be heard says the Lord. Jesus himself got up and went to a desert or a mountain to pray early in the mornings.

Religion vs Spirituality

Religion aims to build one's character. It shapes one's beliefs, attitudes, and actions by giving importance to the adherence of rules. This unites people who share a religion, as they share character traits and outlooks on life. On the other hand, spirituality concentrates more on each person's individual soul.

Spirituality

Spirituality is the recognition of a feeling or sense or belief that there is something greater than oneself. The religious think, that this 'something' is God. Spirituality can be thought of as a manner of pursuing a religious life.

For some people, a spiritual awareness comes after a crisis or traumatic situation on the physical, emotional, or mental level. For others, the call to begin the spiritual journey is triggered by a spontaneous mystical experience or sudden life-changing experience. This awareness is usually forced into the young minds at a very early stage, so it becomes a natural part of their life!

One can be 'spiritual' without being religious.

Spiritual Blindness

A Catholic becomes spiritually blind:

1. When not taking sin seriously.

2. When not knowing what sins he or she is committing.

3. When failing to realise that they are protected by the sacraments they receive.

4. When failing to know the presence of God even when one is sick, distressed, lonely, sorrowful, and so on.

5. When not aware that Jesus came to earth to carry our burden. Believe in him and he will cleanse all sins.

6. When doubting that even after going for confession, that their sins have not been forgiven and continue to suffer guilt.

7. When not aware that the Holy Spirit within us will not allow our hearts to be troubled. He who is inside is greater than the one (the evil one) who is outside!

Soul

Our soul is the part of us that consists of our mind, character, thoughts, and feelings.

The soul is the "driver" in the body the presence of which makes the physical body alive.

Focussing on a holistic education socially, emotionally, spiritually, physically, and culturally is not enough. An important aspect of education must also be its power in the **preparation for life**, *and a life of worth at that – not merely a life of work.*

Basically, the Catholics nourishing their souls through unshakable faith in the Almighty God and prayers, help themselves to lead a life with integrity and happiness.

CHAPTER 3

SOME LIFE-GIVING WORDS FROM THE BIBLE

(The Gospels are the hope of the world)

Although death is the end of physical lives, Catholics see this as a change rather than a complete ending. Following death, God will judge us, and we will go to one (or two) of the three states namely, heaven, hell, and purgatory (a mid-state between heaven and hell!). Catholics pray for those in purgatory so that they can go to heaven as quickly as possible to be with God.

Heaven, Hell, and Purgatory concepts of Catholicism for the human soul after death (when soul leaves the body) is meant to create an awareness of the relative benefits of living a virtuous life as far as is possible, that pleases God, by following Jesus' Life-giving words in the Bible.

When a person truly hears the word of God and receives it into their heart, that word becomes a spiritual seed, quickened by the Holy Spirit, and it produces new life.

The Bible contains many words of Jesus for us `to follow and live a life like that of His, some of which are given below for the purpose of reflection.

Jesus often spoke in parables. Jesus taught the spiritual truths through parables. A parable is a tale about a simple, common subject to illustrate a deeper, valuable moral lesson. There are many parables in the Bible. The parable of the Sower, the parable of the two sons, the parable of the good Samaritan are examples of the parables that Catholics are very familiar with.

There are no parables in the Gospel of John. However, they are in each of the synoptic Gospels, (Gospels with similar contents) Matthew, Mark, and Luke.

Knowing only what Jesus said, is not good enough. One needs to contemplate on, and put all what He said, into practice.

The Old Testament contains the sacred scriptures of the Jewish faith. The New Testament is seen as the fulfilment of the prophecies of the Old Testament. One can see the awesome and wonderful character of God as they become more familiar with each of the 39 books of the Old Testament

NEW TESTAMENT

A Few Words of Jesus – From *the Gospel of Matthew*

1. "Blessed are you when they revile and persecute you and say all kinds of evil against you falsely for My sake. Rejoice and be exceedingly glad, for great is your reward in heaven, for so they persecuted the prophets who were before you." **Matthew 5:11-12**

(Note that **Matthew 5:11-12** means, Matthew Chapter 5, verses 11 to 12)

2. Nor do they light a lamp and put it under a basket, but on a lampstand, and it gives light to all who are in the house. Let your light so shine before men, that they may see your good works and glorify your Father in heaven. **Mathew 5:15-16**

3. Ye have heard that it was said by them of old time, thou shalt not commit adultery: But I say unto you, that whosoever looketh on a woman to lust after her hath committed adultery with her already in his heart. **Mathew 5:27-28**

4. It hath been said, whosoever shall put away his wife, let him give her a writing of divorcement: But I say unto you, that whosoever shall put away his wife, saving for the cause of fornication, causeth her to commit adultery: and whosoever

shall marry her that is divorced committeth adultery. **Mathew 5:31-32**

5. Ye have heard that it hath been said, thou shalt love thy neighbour, and hate thine enemy. But I say unto you, love your enemies, bless them that curse you, do good to them that hate you, and pray for them which despitefully use you, and persecute you; **Matthew 5: 43-44**

6. But thou, when thou prayest, enter into thy closet, and when thou hast shut thy door, pray to thy Father which is in secret; and thy Father which seeth in secret shall reward thee openly. **Matthew 6:6**

7. "For if ye forgive men their trespasses, your heavenly Father will also forgive you: but if ye forgive not men their trespasses, neither will your Father forgive your trespasses." **Matthew 6: 14.15**

8. "But seek ye first the kingdom of God, and his righteousness; and all these things shall be added unto you." Matthew **6:33**

9. "For whosoever shall do the will of my Father which is in heaven, the same is my brother, and sister, and mother." **Matthew 12:50**

10. "Take therefore no thought for the morrow: for the morrow shall take thought for the things of

itself. Sufficient unto the day is the evil thereof." **Matthew 6:34**

11. "Therefore, all things whatsoever ye that men would do to you, do ye even so to them: for this is the law and the prophets." **Matthew 7:12**

12. "Beware of false prophets, which come to you in sheep's clothing, but inwardly they are ravening wolves. Ye shall know them by their fruits. Do men gather grapes of thorns, or figs of thistles." **Matthew 7: 15.16**

13. "Suffer little children, and forbid them not, to come unto me: for of such is the kingdom of heaven." **Matthew 19:14**

14. "The harvest truly is plenteous, but the labourers are few." **Matthew 9:37**

15. "And whosoever shall exalt himself shall be abased; and he that shall humble himself shall be exalted." **Matthew 23:12**

A Few Words of Jesus – From the *Gospel of Mark*

1. "The time is fulfilled, and the kingdom of God is at hand: repent ye and believe the gospel." **Mark 1:15**

2. "Come ye after me, and I will make you to become fishers of men." **Mark 1:17**

3. "And when he had called the people unto him with his disciples also, he said unto them, 'whosoever will come after me, let him deny himself, and take up his cross, and follow me. For whosoever will save his life shall lose it; but whosoever shall lose his life for my sake and the gospel's, the same shall save it.'" **Mark 8:34-35**

4. "Whosoever therefore shall be ashamed of me and of my words in this adulterous and sinful generation; of him also shall the Son of man be ashamed, when he cometh in the glory of his Father with the holy angels." **Mark 8:38**

5. "And whosoever shall offend one of these little ones that believe in me, it is better for him that a millstone were hanged about his neck, and he were cast into the sea." **Mark 9:42**

6. "Jesus beholding him loved him, and said unto him, 'one thing thou lackest: go thy way, sell whatsoever thou hast, and give to the poor, and thou shalt have treasure in heaven: and come, take up the cross, and follow me.'" **Mark 10:21**

7. "And Jesus looking upon them saith, 'with men it is impossible, but not with God: for with God all things are possible.'" **Mark 10:27**

8. "The Son of man came not to be ministered unto, but to minister, and to give his life a ransom for many." **Mark 10: 45**

9. "Therefore, I say unto you, what things soever ye desire, when ye pray, believe that ye receive them, and ye shall have them. And when ye stand praying, forgive, if ye have ought against any: that your Father also which is in heaven may forgive you your trespasses." **Mark 11:24-25**

10. "And he said unto them, 'Go ye into all the world, and preach the gospel to every creature'". **Mark 16:15**

A Few Words of Jesus – From the *Gospel of Luke*

1. "And he said unto them, 'I must preach the kingdom of God to other cities also: for therefore am I sent.'" **Luke 4:43**

2. "And Jesus answering said unto them, 'They that are whole need not a physician; but they that are sick. I came not to call the righteous, but sinners to repentance.'" **Luke 5:31-32**

3. Jesus taught the following 8 **beatitudes** to a crowd.

    i. Blessed *are* the poor in spirit: for theirs is the kingdom of heaven.

    ii. Blessed *are* they that mourn for they shall be comforted.

- iii. Blessed *are* the meek: for they shall inherit the earth.
- iv. Blessed *are* they which do hunger and thirst after righteousness: for they shall be filled.
- v. Blessed *are* the merciful: for they shall obtain mercy.
- vi. Blessed *are* the pure in heart: for they shall see God.
- vii. Blessed *are* the peacemakers: for they shall be called the children of God.
- viii. Blessed *are* they which are persecuted for righteousness' sake: for theirs is the kingdom of heaven. **Luke 6:20–23**.

4. "Then he called his twelve disciples together, and gave them power and authority over all devils, and to cure diseases. And he sent them to preach the kingdom of God, and to heal the sick. And he said unto them, 'Take nothing for your journey, neither staves, nor scrip, neither bread, neither money; neither have two coats apiece. And whatsoever house ye enter into, there abide, and thence depart. And whosoever will not receive you, when ye go out of that city, shake off the very dust from your feet for a testimony against them. And they

departed, and went through the towns, preaching the gospel, and healing everywhere.'" **Luke 9:1-6**

5. "The apostle John said to Jesus, 'we saw a man driving out demons in your name and we tried to stop him, because he is not one of us.' Do not stop him, Jesus said, 'for whoever is not against you is for you.'" **Luke 9: 49-50**

6. "And behold, a certain lawyer stood up, and tempted him, saying, 'Master, what shall I do to inherit eternal life?' He said unto him, 'what is written in the law? how readest thou?' And he answering said, 'Thou shalt love the Lord thy God with all thy heart, and with all thy soul, and with all thy strength, and with all thy mind; and thy neighbour as thyself.' And he said unto him, 'thou hast answered right: this do, and thou shalt live.'" **Luke 10: 25-28**

7. "And I say unto you, Ask, and it shall be given you; seek, and ye shall find; knock, and it shall be opened unto you." **Luke 11:9-1**

8. "And it came to pass, as he spoke these things, a certain woman of the company lifted up her voice, and said unto him, 'Blessed is the womb that bare thee, and the paps which thou hast sucked.' But he said, Yea rather, blessed are they that hear the word of God, and keep it." **Luke 11:27-28**

9. "And the apostles said unto the Lord, 'Increase our faith.' And the Lord said, 'If ye had faith as a grain of mustard seed, ye might say unto this

sycamine tree, be thou plucked up by the root, and be thou planted in the sea; and it should obey you.'" **Luke 17:5-6**

10. "Whosoever shall seek to save his life shall lose it; and whosoever shall lose his life shall preserve it." **Luke 17:33**

11. "And it came to pass, that on one of those days, as he taught the people in the temple, and preached the gospel, the chief priests and the scribes came upon him with the elders, And spoke unto him, saying, 'Tell us, by what authority doest thou these things? or who is he that gave thee this authority?' And he answered and said unto them, 'I will also ask you one thing; and answer me: The baptism of John, was it from heaven, or of men?'

And they reasoned with themselves, saying, 'If we shall say, from heaven; he will say, why then believed ye him not? But and if we say, of men; all the people will stone us: for they be persuaded that John was a prophet.' And they answered that they could not tell whence it was.

And Jesus said unto them, 'Neither tell I you by what authority I do these things.'" **Luke 20:1-8**

12. "Then said he unto them, 'Nation shall rise against nation, and kingdom against kingdom.'" **Luke 21:10**

A Few Words of Jesus – From the *Gospel of John*

1. "All that the Father giveth me shall come to me; and him that cometh to me I will in no wise cast out. For I came down from heaven, not to do mine own will, but the will of him that sent me. And this is the Father's will which hath sent me, that of all which he hath given me I should lose nothing but should raise it up again at the last day. And this is the will of him that sent me, that everyone which seeth the Son, and believeth on him, may have everlasting life: and I will raise him up at the last day." **John 6:37-40**

2. "I am the living bread which came down from heaven: if any man eats of this bread, he shall live for ever: and the bread that I will give is my flesh, which I will give for the life of the world." **John 6:51**

3. "For my flesh is meat indeed, and my blood is drink indeed. He that eateth my flesh, and drinketh my blood, dwelleth in me, and I in him." **John 6: 55-56**

4. "Ye judge after the flesh; I judge no man. And yet if I judge, my judgment is true: for I am not alone, but I and the Father that sent me" **John 10:10-11**

5. "I am the door: by me if any man enters in, he shall be saved, and shall go in and out, and find pasture. The thief cometh not, but for to steal, and to kill, and to destroy; I am come that they might have life, and that they might have it more abundantly." **John 10:9-10**

6. "My sheep hear my voice, and I know them, and they follow me: And I give unto them eternal life; and they shall never perish, neither shall any man pluck them out of my hand. My Father, which gave them me, is greater than all; and no man is able to pluck them out of my Father's hand. I and my Father are one." **John 10:27-30**

7. "And if any man hears my words, and believe not, I judge him not: for I came not to judge the world, but to save the world." **John 12:47**

8. "A new commandment I give unto you, that ye love one another; as I have loved you, that ye also love one another. By this shall all men know that ye are my disciples, if ye have love, one to another."
John 13:34-35

9. "Jesus saith unto him, I am the way, the truth, and the life: no man cometh unto the Father, but by me." **John 14:6**

10. "He that hath my commandments, and keepeth them, he it is that loveth me: and he that loveth me shall be loved of my Father, and I will love him, and will manifest myself to him." **John 14:21**

11. "I am the vine, ye are the branches: He that abideth in me, and I in him, the same bringeth forth much fruit: for without me ye can do nothing." **John 15:5**

12. "Greater love hath no man than this, that a man lay down his life for his friends." **John 15:13**

13. "If the world hates you, ye know that it hated me before it hated you." **John 15:18**

Extracts from the various letters of Paul, the apostle to the early Christians.

1. "Know that for those who love God all things work together for good, for those who are called according to His purpose." **Romans 8:28**

2. "Let no man despise thy youth; but be thou an example of the believers, in word, in conversation, in charity, in spirit, in faith, in purity." **1 Timothy 4:12**

3. "The Spirit also helps in our weaknesses. For we do not know what we should pray for as we ought, but the Spirit Himself makes intercession for us with groanings which cannot be uttered." **Romans 8:26**

4. "Now I beseech you, brethren, by the name of our Lord Jesus Christ, that ye all speak the same thing, and that there be no divisions among you; but that ye be perfectly joined together in the same mind and in the same judgment." **1 Corinthians 1:10**

5. "I have been crucified with Christ; it is no longer I who live, but Christ lives in me; and the life which I now live in the flesh I live by faith in the Son of God who loved me and gave Himself for me." **Galatians 2:20**

A Few Verses from The Old Testament

1. "God says to 'fear not, for I am with you; be not dismayed, for I am your God; I will strengthen you, I will help you, I will uphold you with my righteous right hand.'" **Isaiah 41:10**

2. "For the Lord God is a Sun and Shield; the Lord bestows favour and honour. No good thing does he withhold from those who walk uprightly." **Psalm 84:11**

3. "Then the king commanded, and Daniel was brought and cast into the den of lions. The king declared to Daniel, 'May your God, whom you serve continually, deliver you!'" **Daniel 6:16**

4. "'The days are coming,' declares the Sovereign Lord, 'when I will send a famine through the land – not a famine of food or a thirst for water, but a famine of hearing the words of the Lord.'" **Amos 8:11**

5. "The Spirit of the Sovereign Lord is on me, because the Lord has anointed me to proclaim good news to the poor. He has sent me to bind up the broken-

hearted, to proclaim freedom for the captives and release from darkness for the prisoners." **Isaiah 61:1**

6. "He has shown all you people what is good. And what does the Lord require of you? To act justly and to love mercy and to walk humbly with your God."
Micah 6:8

7. "'Surely the day is coming; it will burn like a furnace. All the arrogant and every evildoer will be stubble, and the day that is coming will set them on fire,' says the Lord Almighty. 'Not a root or a branch will be left to them.'" **Malachi 4:1**

8. "The Lord forgave David's sins and made him a glorious king, and he also promised that the kings of Israel would be David's descendants for all time."
Sirach 47:11

9. "I will give you a new heart and put a new spirit in you; I will remove from you your heart of stone and give you a heart of flesh." **Ezekiel 36:26**

10. "But he knows the way that I take; when he has tested me, I will come forth as gold." **Job 27:10**

The Scriptures – The Sacred Writings

The Bible is not a novel. It contains the word of God. It is a 'breathing book' – it guides our life. We have to breathe the word of God into us by reading the scriptures every day.

One of the many ways to hear the word of God is through the scriptures. Scriptures are the sacred writings of a religion. All scripture is inspired by God and is useful for teaching, for correction and for training in righteousness (right living) so that everyone who belongs to God may be proficient and equipped for living such a life and for doing good deeds.

STRIVE TO EMBRACE THE SHINING LIFE

CHAPTER 4

PROCLAIMING THE GOOD NEWS

What is the ardour of the Catholic Church? It is the story of life, death, and resurrection of Jesus – It is the **good news** that needs to be proclaimed.

Broadly speaking, anything that involves sharing the Catholic faith and bringing others to know Christ and his Church is part of the work of Proclamation.

Jesus himself commanded us to spread the Good News. All around us are people who have never heard about Jesus who desires abundant life for them. They need to hear this good news.

Proclamation calls each Catholic to spread the Gospel - the story of who Jesus is and what He did. In a special way, proclamation is focused on 're-proposing' the Gospel (the life and teaching of Jesus) to those who have experienced a crisis of faith due to indifference to or rejection of the Catholic Faith for some reason!

Proclamation simply means sharing the Gospel of Jesus Christ with others so that they may make the decision to follow Jesus, become His disciples, and join His Holy Catholic Church if they so desire.

Proclamation in modern times is the same as in the past years but using newer methods and newer expressions.

Many young people today are indifferent to Catholic faith for various reasons, but one thing is certain: They are immersed in a culture that has deprived them of the opportunity to encounter the Truth.

There has been therefore, in recent times, a breakdown in the way Catholics pass down their faith to the young. This has led not only to a degree of exodus to other faith communities but also to a "void" before commencing their search for the meaning of life.

The young need answers to their questions where they could see God, why He allows sufferings in the world and so on.

The Catholic Church in a country also sends people called **missionaries,** to spread the good news to people in other countries.

There appears to be a growing slackness in people's willingness to devote their time freely to their Parishes. This causes a great challenge to the Church authorities in providing a structured service.

The Catholic Parishes are in need of a renewed missionary dynamism. People, nowadays, are reluctant to take responsibility, mainly due to the fear of losing their free time to do other things which they enjoy a lot. More motivation and spirituality are required to undertake the necessary pastoral work and make it pleasurable and meaningful.

Proclamation using old methods in the new age will end up in creating a lot of uneasiness in people. People are far more educated now and they need new methods of convincing them of the merits of another faith than that which they are familiar with. In the past, those who succumbed to conversion were the poor, downtrodden, marginalized and the suppressed.

Again, why would people of other faiths, who are happy with them, need a change. All faiths aim to find solace to their souls and people appear to be happy with the way they go about with their spirituality.

Catholicism has the specific focus of introducing God and Saviour Jesus Christ to people.

The common methods used for proclamation fall into:

1. **Open-air preaching** (also called street preaching or public preaching), is the act of proclaiming a religious faith in public places.

2. **Preaching through a sermon** in churches or any building to a group of people through a short homily or a straightforward guide to life-giving words of Jesus.

3. **"Lifestyle evangelism"** strategy that focuses on living a holy, winsome Christlike life among unbelievers with the goal of attracting people to the message of Jesus Christ.

4. **Friendship proclamation** whereby those who preach try to be friends with people who want to hear the good news.

5. **Preaching to children** where catechists, youth ministers etc. reach out to children in schools and churches.

The six valuable comments stated below in connection with the *spreading of Good News* are taken from Pope Francis' book **Evangelii Gaudium**:

1. "To pray for a person with whom one is irritated is a beautiful step forward in love" is evangelisation.

2. "The women make indispensable contribution to society through the sensitivity, intuition and other distinctive skill sets which they, more than men tend to possess. Many women share pastoral responsibilities with priests, helping to guide people, families and groups and offering new contributions to theological reflection."

3. "Youth ministry, as traditionally organised, has suffered the impact of social changes. Young people often fail to find responses to their concerns, needs, problems and hurts in the usual structures. Adults find it hard to listen patiently to them, to appreciate their concerns and demands, and to speak to them in a language they can understand. For the same reason, their efforts in the field of education do

not produce the results expected. The rise and growth of associations and movements mostly made up of young people can be seen as the work of the Holy Spirit, who blazes new trails to meet their expectations and their search for a deep spirituality and a more real sense of belonging. There remains a need, however, to ensure that these associations actively participate in the Church's overall pastoral efforts."

4. Many places are experiencing a dearth of vocations to the priesthood and consecrated life. This is often to a lack of contagious apostolic fervour in communities which results in a cooling of enthusiasm and attractiveness.

Wherever there is life, fervour, and desire to bring Christ to others, genuine vocations will arise.

Even in parishes where priests are not particularly committed or joyful, the fraternal life and fervour of the community can awaken in the young, a desire to consecrate themselves completely to God and to the preaching of the Gospel. This is particularly true if such a living community prays insistently for vocations and courageously proposes to its young people the path of special consecration.

On the other hand, despite the scarcity of vocations, today we are increasingly aware of the need for a better process of selecting candidates to the priesthood. Seminaries cannot accept candidates on the basis of any motivation whatsoever, especially if those motivations have to do with affective insecurity or the pursuit of power, human glory, or economic well-being.

5. "It is helpful to listen to young people and elderly. Both represent a source of hope for every people. The elderly brings with them memory and the wisdom of experience which warns us not to foolishly repeat our past mistakes. Young people call us to renewed and expansive hope, for they represent new directions for humanity and open us up to the future, lest we cling to a nostalgia for structures and customs which are no longer life-giving in today's world".

6. "The homily is the touchstone for judging a priest's closeness and ability to communicate to his people. The faithful attach great importance to it, and that both they and their ordained ministers suffer because of homilies – the laity having to listen to them and the clergy from having to preach them. It is sad that this is the case. The homily can be an intense and happy

experience of the Spirit, a consoling encounter with God's word, a constant source of renewal and growth.

The homily cannot be a form of entertainment like those presented by media, yet it does need to give life and meaning to the celebration.

It is a distinctive genre, since it is preaching which is situated within the framework of *liturgical* celebration; hence it should be brief and avoid taking on the semblance of a speech or a lecture.

The words of the preacher must be measured, so that the Lord, more than his minister, will be the centre of attention".

Atheists are not necessarily opposed to believing in God. They simply can't believe without sufficient reason or without objective facts".

A testimony, like the one below, from a converted atheist that introduced Jesus to him is heart-warming:

"I have followed your advice regarding how to read Jesus' Words and already feel a very strong connection with my faith and that my relationship with Jesus is solid. This is in large part due to your tutelage, although admittedly God did most."

Because of widespread ethical concerns, organisations must also show interest in the concept of workplace spirituality. It involves the effort to find one's ultimate purpose in life, to develop a strong connection to co-workers and other people associated with work, and to have consistency (or alignment) between one's core beliefs and the values of their organization.

The following are some areas where proclamation will be very helpful, especially to the young ones.

- Science and religion
- Evil in the world
- The Church and the unbelieving world
- Atheists, non-believers, and non-practicing Catholic Christians.

Some examples of doing this could include:

- Giving love to those who are vulnerable.
- Allowing the poor, a dignified life.
- Stopping the spread of imperfect knowledge of the Catholic Faith.
- Helping people to have a deep understanding of God and His ways.
- Respecting the advice of the clergy, the teachers, and parents.

CHAPTER 5

MARY AND THE SAINTS

Mother Mary

Mary, mother of Jesus was the adopted child of Joachim and Anne. Mary lived in Nazareth and was betrothed to Joseph, a long-time widower. At the time of her betrothal to Joseph, Mary was about 13 years old. Mary lived for 11 years after the death of her son Jesus, dying in 41 AD.

Mary continued her prayerful life after the ascension of Jesus into heaven.

Mary had a natural death and was then taken up bodily into heaven (**The Assumption**).

Mary was present at a wedding in Cana where Jesus turned water into wine after Mary told him that more wine was required for the wedding guests; she was also at the foot of the Cross at his crucifixion when Jesus told her to take John, the apostle into her household as her son.

Pope Pius IX declared that the most Blessed Virgin Mary, in the first instance of her conception was preserved free from all stain of original sin. It is a doctrine revealed by God and therefore to be believed firmly and constantly by all Catholics.

Mary was more than just a saint. In popular devotion she is always dressed in blue. She is called by a number of titles such as the 'star of the sea' (*Stella Maris*), Lady of Fatima and many more.

We all pray but the prayer of the righteous is powerful and effective. Thus, the prayers of holy people who are canonised as saints by the Catholic Church are effective. For this reason, we ask them to intercede for us in our prayers.

A person can be an intercessor for another. We are all intercessors for each other. That is why we can pray for each other.

Most people fail to understand that dead people for the humans are living people for God. During the transfiguration of Jesus for example, Moses and Elijah who were dead long time ago were talking to Jesus!

Mother Mary had given apparitions in several places like Tepeyac Hill (in a suburb of Mexico City), Rwanda, Fatima, Medjugorje and so on. This couldn't be if she is dead!

In the apparition in Fatima, On May 13, 1917, the three children – Lucia, Jacinta and Francisco took their flock of sheep to a natural hollow in the ground known as the Cova da Iria to graze, just outside the town of Fatima in Portugal, and Mary appeared to them.

Lucia was then only nine years old; Jacinta was six and Francisco was eight.

In each of her apparitions, Mary had a message to deliver to the world.

The Catholic Church is very careful when it comes to approving and recognizing Marian apparitions. There are about 26 approved apparitions.

Mary is interested in God's people, and she intercedes for them. Since Mary is the mother of Jesus, and Jesus is the head of the Catholic Church, Mary is called the Mother of the Catholic Church.

Veneration (or respect) is different from worship. Respect is a feeling of deep admiration for someone, or something elicited by their abilities, qualities, or achievements. Worship, on the other hand, refers to a higher respect and greater esteem.

Catholics venerate Mary but do not worship her. They also do not worship the statues of Mary and saints when they look at or touch them. The honour rendered to an image through veneration passes to its prototype. The honour paid to a statue is a "respectful veneration" and not adoration which is due to God alone.

Two tablets of the Law given to Moses by God was housed in a gold-plated wooden chest in biblical times. It was called the **Ark of the Covenant** and it rested in the ' Holy of Holies' inside the Tabernacle of the ancient Temple of Jerusalem and was seen only by the high priest of the Israelites. The 'Holy of Holies' is a term in the Hebrew Bible that refers to the inner sanctuary of the Tabernacle, where God's presence appeared.

The catholic church refers to Mother Mary as the Ark of the Covenant in the New Testament because she is the vessel that carried Jesus!

Further, the glory of Lord Jesus encompasses Mother Mary. This why the Catholics honour Mary.

As everyone knows, the good news that a saviour was to be born for the salvation of humanity through Mary was announced to her by Angel Gabriel.

An angel appeared to Mary and said:

> *"Hail Mary,*
> *Full of Grace,*
> *The Lord is with thee.*
> *Blessed art thou among women,*
> *and blessed is the fruit*
> *of thy womb, Jesus".*

As a second part to this prayer, other words were added by the Catholic Church as follows:

> *Holy Mary,*
> *Mother of God,*
> *pray for us sinners now,*
> *and at the hour of our death.*
> *Amen.*

The Rosary

In saying the Rosary Catholics call to mind, 20 Mysteries. There are **5** events/mysteries for each of: Joyful, the Sorrowful, the Glorious and the Luminous Mysteries. There are other prayers also said when praying the Rosary. These are the Apostles Creed, Our Father (Lord's Prayer), Hail Mary, and Glory Be (Glory Be to the Father, and to the Son, and to the Holy Spirit. As it was in the beginning, is now, and ever shall be, world without end).

The rosary begins with the recitation of the Apostle's Creed, an Our Father, three Hail Mary's and a Glory Be. Then there are five decades which each begin and end with an Our Father and Glory Be and have ten Hail Mary's in between. When praying the rosary, one meditates on the events in Jesus' life.

After each 'Glory be" it is now the custom to say the following prayer:

> **O my Jesus**, forgive us our sins,
> save us from the fires of hell; lead all souls to heaven especially those who are in most need of. Your mercy.

The four mysteries with the twenty events cover the Life of our Lord Jesus Christ and the Coronation of the

Blessed Virgin Mary. Mother Mary is called the Queen of Heaven and Earth by the Catholic Church.

The Rosary focuses on key aspects of the Catholic faith, especially as seen in the twenty mysteries. The events around the Joyful Mysteries are:

- the **Annunciation**
- the **Visitation**
- the **Nativity**
- the **Presentation of the Child Jesus**
- the **Finding of the Child Jesus in the Temple**

The Sorrowful Mysteries consist of the following five events:

- Christ's **Agony in the Garden**
- the **Scourging**
- the **Crowning of Thorns**
- the **Carrying of the Cross**
- the **Crucifixion**

The Glorious Mysteries include the five events:

- the **Resurrection**
- the **Ascension**
- the **Descent of the Holy Spirit**
- the **Assumption of Mary**
- the **Coronation of Mary**

Finally, the Luminous Mysteries (or Mysteries of Light) comprise the five events:

- the **Baptism of Jesus**
- the **Wedding at Cana**
- the **Proclamation of the Kingdom**
- the **Transfiguration**
- the **Institution of the Eucharist**

After completion of the first decade for one event of a given mystery, another event is called to mind, and the process of prayer continues. The beads in the Rosary help to keep count of the ten Hail Marys for each event of a mystery.

The rosary is a devotion in honour of the Virgin Mary.

When the angel appeared to a shepherd, it said "Go into the world and proclaim the good news to the whole of creation"

Each time the Catholics say the Rosary, they are reminding themselves of the Good News. Praying the Rosary is also a powerful protection for them.

The Rosary is the most powerful weapon against the evil one. It is referred to as **Mary's sword**.

Like the way Jesus repeated His prayers in the Gethsemane Garden, "Hail Mary" is also repeated.

Mother Mary is expected to be used in the second coming of Jesus also. The Catholics firmly believe that they can go to Jesus through Mary!

Jesus honoured Mary as the Queen of heaven.

According to Catholic tradition, the Rosary was instituted by the Blessed Virgin Mary herself. In the 13th century, she is said to have appeared to **St. Dominic** (founder of the Dominicans), given him a rosary, and asked that Christians pray the Hail Mary, Our Father and 'Glory Be' prayers.

The Bible does "not" mention the Rosary because this form of prayer originated only during the Middle Ages.

Devotion to the Rosary is one of the most distinguishable features of popular Catholic spirituality. The Rosary inspires Catholics to meditate on the mysteries of the lives of Jesus and Mary. Meditation is an important part of the lives of Catholics. According to the Catechism of the Catholic Church, meditation "engages thought, imagination, emotion, and desire. This mobilization of faculties is necessary in order to deepen our convictions of faith, prompt the conversion of our heart and strengthen our will to follow Christ."

The Rosary is a meditative prayer based on Scripture. When we pray the Rosary, we ask Mary to pray for us as we seek to grow closer to her son Jesus by contemplating His life, death, and Resurrection.

Different mysteries for different days

- **Mondays:** say the Joyful mystery.
- **Tuesdays and Fridays:** say the sorrowful mystery.
- **Wednesdays, Saturdays, and Sundays**: say the glorious mystery.
- **Thursdays:** say the Luminous mystery.

At the end of the Rosary, the following prayer is recited:

Hail Holy Queen

Hail Holy Queen, Mother of Mercy, our Life, our Sweetness, and our hope. To thee we cry, poor banished children of Eve. To thee we send up our sighs, mourning and weeping in this vale of tears. Turn then most gracious advocate, thine eyes of mercy toward us, and after this, our exile, show unto us, the blessed fruit of thy womb, Jesus. O clement, O loving, O sweet Virgin Mary. Pray for us O Holy Mother of God, that we may be made worthy of the promises of Christ.

Let us pray. O God, whose only begotten Son, by His life, death, and resurrection, has purchased for us the rewards of eternal life; grant, we beseech Thee, that meditating upon these mysteries of the Most Holy Rosary of the Blessed Virgin Mary, we may imitate what they contain and obtain what they promise, through the same Christ Our Lord.
Amen.

(End the reciting of the rosary by making the sign of the cross.)

Honouring Vs Worshiping

Catholics love and honour Mary, their heavenly mother. They give her respect and reverence as the mother of God. They recognize Mary as the Mother of the Church—Mother of Salvation—for guiding the Church and leading each of her faithful into a closer relationship with her son, Jesus Christ. It is only God that Catholics worship.

Feast Days of Mother Mary

There are many Marian feast days celebrated in the Catholic Church, but the principal ones are:

- the Immaculate Conception
- the Solemnity of Mary
- the Annunciation
- the Coronation of Mary, and the
- Assumption of Mary into heaven.

The Immaculate Conception is the belief that the Virgin Mary was free of original sin from the moment of her conception.

The Solemnity of Mary is a feast day for the Blessed Virgin Mary to honour her motherhood of Jesus Christ, Son of God.

The annunciation commemorates the announcement by the angel Gabriel to the Virgin Mary that she would conceive a son by the power of the Holy Spirit to be called Jesus.

The idea that the Virgin Mother of God was physically crowned as Queen of Heaven after her Assumption is a traditional Catholic belief echoed in the Rosary.

Assumption of Mary into heaven commemorates the belief that when Mary, the mother of Jesus Christ, died, her body was "assumed" into heaven to be reunited with her soul, instead of going through the natural process of physical decay upon death.

Memorare

A Catholic prayer seeking the intercession of the blessed virgin Mary is as follows:

Remember, O' most gracious Virgin Mary, that never was it known that anyone who fled to thy protection, implored thy help, or sought thy intercession was left unaided.

Inspired with this confidence, I fly to thee, O' Virgin of Virgins, my mother.

To thee do I come, before thee I stand, sinful and sorrowful.

O' mother of the world incarnate, despise not my petitions, but in thy mercy hear and answer me.

THE SAINTS

Saints are holy men and women who had died on earth but are alive in heaven. Saints can help us out a lot by their intercession with God. This is the reason why Catholics pray

The Catholic Church describes everyone who is in heaven as saint.

Although the Catholic Church has fixed a calendar day to remember each saint, November 1 is assigned to celebrate all the saints. It is thus called the "All Saints Day"

One doesn't have to be a perfect person to be a saint.

A person after their death may be declared a saint by the Catholic Church through a process called Canonisation.

Canonisation means recognising whether someone is worthy enough to be put on a formal list of saints. The process of Canonisation is amazingly complicated.

There are four steps in Canonisation:

   i. Ensuring a candidate is a complete servant of God
  ii. Verifying that the candidate is venerable.
 iii. Conferring on the candidate the title "Blessed"
  iv. Declaring the candidate as a saint in a ceremony.

The first process is carried out by the local diocese of the candidate. The findings are then sent to Vatican where it is reviewed by the Congregation for the Causes of Saints. If approved, the candidate is declared a servant of God.

The second step is to verify that that the candidate manifested heroic virtues that reflect the Gospel and if so, the person is recognised as venerable.

The third step is to declare the person, **blessed**. To do this, scientists, doctors, and theologians look into the validity of a miracle attributed to the candidate. A ceremony called Beatification takes place and after that the 'blessed' can be venerated. In the case of a martyr, a miracle is not necessary.

In the fourth step, the 'blessed' must perform a second miracle before they can be declared a saint. This declaration by the Catholic Church happens at a Canonisation Ceremony at St. Peter's Square in Rome.

Whatever traits the holy men and women had to become saints; God makes His presence knows through them.

There are over 3000 people who had been canonised as saints since the time the Catholic Church started recognising men and women who impressed the world while tirelessly endured life-threatening illnesses, humiliation, torture etc. to make God known to the world.

Patron Saints

Many saints are venerated for a more specific reason. These saints came to be known as patron saints. Some saints are considered patron saints of nations, cities, or other geographical areas. Others were adopted by members of a particular guild or profession.

Saint Joseph, the foster father of Jesus, for example, is the Patron Saint of workers. The world celebrates this patron on May 1 each year!

Veneration of Saints

The Catholics believe in venerating saints. The saints followed God's will with great love and heroic virtue—often in the face of persecution. Veneration is shown outwardly by respectfully bowing or making the sign of the cross before a saint's icon, relics, or statue, or by going on pilgrimage to sites associated with saints.

The Catholics believe also in the Communion of Saints and ask them to intercede with God and pray for them just as they ask their friends on earth to pray for them.

All the saints are still alive and are united with us through Jesus. All our family members or friends who followed Jesus but have died are still united to us. The closer we get to Jesus, the closer we get to everyone united to him. That's the communion of saints!

CHAPTER 6

A GLIMPSE INTO THE HOLY LAND

When in high school, learning Physics, Chemistry and other sciences, a student in class became all the more clear about a concept taught when seeing it in context in a practical session. Concepts which were believable, true but still somewhat abstract suddenly comes into sharper focus when seeing the concepts in real life. The teachings of the Bible are not so different. The concepts that Jesus taught are very real and have depth for many people in everyday life. Yet for over long years they may remain slightly abstract. To see them in a practical session could make better sense of those teachings.

The Bible is a book that holds a never-ending litany of truths. Occasionally a film, made to represent a chapter of the Bible, will add some colour and depth to these truths. What if one could travel back in time and experience part of the Bible's teachings?

Many people make a pilgrimage to the Holy Land, that serves as a practical session with time travel, covering life's greatest subject, the Word of God. These people are very privileged indeed

The Holy Land is a sizeable country, and it spans many centuries of history. I am sure one could spend decades there and still have several lifetimes' worth of learning to absorb. Between the Old and New Testaments, there are hundreds of places to visit. The pilgrims experience at least some of the main themes in Jesus' life.

"By going to the Holy Land, the Holy Land becomes real in the life of Christians because of what it stands for, said Pope Paul VI. He said that it is the **'fifth gospel'** which is not written in ink but written on stones."

The Holy Land includes Israel, the Palestinian territories, and parts of Lebanon, Jordan, and Syria.

The narration below follows chronologically the life of Jesus in his short time on earth.

Bethlehem
The Birthplace of Jesus

The town of Bethlehem is small, humble, and one of the best-known places in the Christian world. It lies surprisingly close to Jerusalem, a mere 15 minutes' drive from the centre of the holy city, separated by an imposing grey wall decorated with barbed wire and punctuated by machine gun turrets. Now part of the infamous West Bank in the Gaza Strip, Bethlehem still carries a sense of humility and strife, and it is easy to see the simplicity of a village that Jesus chose for his humble beginnings.

The Church of Nativity, within which the grotto lies, is quiet on some days! The church has suffered in the intervening years and bears the scars of historical battles and atrocities. Still, there is a quiet and understated splendour about it, as if it carries with pride its immortality at hosting the first coming of the Son of God.

Nearby, the Shepherds' Fields of Bethlehem (an area to the east traditionally believed to be the area that the shepherds kept "watch over their flocks by night") remain as pastureland, although housing developments are beginning to close in. Several small churches have been built over the years to commemorate the event, some over each other in the intervening centuries. Even today, local shepherds can be seen on the pastureland.

The manger in which Jesus was laid is placed within a small and dark grotto, through which crowds of people surge, paying homage to the spot that graces many of our Christmas carols.

During his preaching days Jesus used a shepherd's life to illustrate his relationship with his disciples. As He said, He is the shepherd, and He knows His flock and the flock knows Him. According to the Gospel of Luke, Jesus' parents lived in Nazareth, but travelled to Bethlehem for the census of AD 6, and that Jesus was subsequently born there. Matthew reported that Herod the Great, when advised that a 'King of the Jews' had been born in Bethlehem, ordered the killing of all the children aged two and under in the town and surrounding areas. The Bible tells us that Jesus' earthly father, Joseph, is warned of this in a dream. We know that he shepherds his new family to Egypt, and only returns after Herod dies. However, Joseph is warned in another dream not to return to the region of Judea, and so he chose to bring the family back to the region of Galilee, and the town of Nazareth.

Baby Jesus and his mother Mary are the central figures of the Christmas story. Mary and her betrothed husband Joseph left their home in Nazareth to travel to Joseph's ancestral home, Bethlehem. Finding no place to stay in the town, Mary gave birth to Jesus in the primitive lodgings of an animal stable, referred to as Jesus' manger. Jesus and Mary were visited by shepherds, and the three wise men who travelled long distances to witness the fulfilment of an ancient prophesy.

Jesus is also called **Christ**; "Christ" means "the anointed one". There is no evidence concerning the month or day of Jesus' birth. The date of 25th December was fixed arbitrarily. The exact date is not important. What is important is that *Jesus was born to redeem mankind.*

Nazareth
The Place Where Jesus Grew Up

The town of Nazareth is a surprisingly large, sprawling community, spread generously over picturesque hills to the north of Israel and located in a pleasant, high and natural bowl in the local geography. It is here that Jesus grew up and lived until he was 30. It was here too that his mother, Mary, was informed of her immaculate conception by an Angel of God before her trip with Joseph to Bethlehem.

Over 2000 years later, it is not difficult to see the Nazareth of the Bible in the narrow streets nestled in the folds of the hills. It is not difficult to see a bustling town and a roaring trade for carpenters and builders, as Joseph and Jesus were. Nazareth has not rushed to meet the twenty first century. The town is peppered with greenery and the buildings are low and modest. It retains a wholesome and honest air about it, but there is a strong undercurrent of commerce. The town is largely Arab, and its centre is bustling. Nazareth is rich with shrines, chapels, churches, and other signs of Christian worship. Churches dedicated to Mary and Joseph celebrate the family that marked a new chapter in God's dynasty.

Nazareth's fame is uncharted before the time of Jesus. Even during Jesus' life on earth, Nazareth's fame was limited. Jesus' teachings had an ominous start here, with the people of Nazareth nearly ending his life when he began proclaiming his divine heritage. It prompted the saying, by Luke and others, that "no prophet is accepted in his own, native place." This is an unsurprising reaction from a population that must have seen Jesus grow up, for 30 years, as an ordinary boy and an ordinary man, and his proclamations must have sounded heretic. Despite its low standing in the Bible, Nazareth offers a great deal for tourists and pilgrims. Although not very famous for the divine works of Jesus during his lifetime, the intervening centuries have seen devotees from all over the world create testaments to the family home of Jesus. An area dedicated to showing visitors what life looked like in Jesus' time proves an effective window into the pages of the *Bible*. Typical houses and their architecture, the tools of a New Testament carpenter and builder, farm layouts and communal wells, olive presses and a historian's recount of the daily routines of townspeople of that era bring context to the setting of many stories in the Bible.

For many people today, personal identity and fulfilment depend upon being well-known, acknowledged and in demand. Jesus was historically invisible for 90 percent of his life, leaving no footprint of who he was or what he did during those years.

Luke writes that every year Joseph and Mary made the 150-mile roundtrip from Nazareth to Jerusalem to celebrate the Feast of Passover. When Jesus was twelve years old, about twenty miles into the return trip home to Nazareth, his parents discovered that Jesus was missing from their caravan of family and friends. Any parent can imagine the terror that they must have felt when they couldn't find their son. After a second day to return to Jerusalem, on the third day they found the boy Jesus in the temple, "sitting among the teachers, listening to them and asking them questions." When Mary rebuked him, it became apparent that Jesus was not accidentally lost, but that he had deliberately stayed behind: "Didn't you know that I had to be in my Father's house?" Mary and Joseph did not understand this mysterious response. After their safe return to Nazareth, Jesus "was obedient to them and He grew in wisdom and stature and in favour with God and man".

Jesus first learned, prayed, and later preached as a young man in a Synagogue. A church called the Synagogue Church was built above the original location of the Roman period synagogue. It is in the middle of Nazareth's old market.

A church was established at the site where, according to Roman Catholic tradition, the Annunciation took place. Greek Orthodox tradition holds that this event occurred while Mary was drawing water from a local spring in Nazareth, and the Greek Orthodox Church of the Annunciation was erected at that alternate site.

The Church of the Annunciation was founded around the same time as the Church of the Nativity (the birthplace) and the Church of the Holy Sepulchre (the tomb). The story of the Annunciation is as follows.

Many years before, God had sent an angel, Gabriel, to Nazareth. The angel had a message for a young woman (Mary), promised in marriage to a man named Joseph, who was a descendent of King David. Her name was Mary. The angel came to her and said, **"Peace be with you! The Lord is with you and has greatly blessed you!"**

Mary was deeply troubled by the angel's message, and she wondered what his words meant. The angel said to her, "Don't be afraid, Mary; God has been gracious to you. You will become pregnant and give birth to a son, and you will name him Jesus. He will be great and will be called the son of the Most High God. The Lord God will make him a king, as his ancestor David was, and will be the king of the descendants of Jacob forever; his kingdom will never end!"

Mary said to the angel "I am a virgin. How, then, can this be?" The angel answered, "**The Holy Spirit** will come on you, and God's power will rest upon you. For this reason the holy child will be called the Son of God. Remember your relative Elizabeth. It is said that she cannot have children, but she herself is now six months pregnant, even though she is very old. For there is nothing God cannot do." "I am the Lord's servant," said Mary; "may it happen to me as you have said." And the angel left her. The dwelling of the Holy Family, in the times of Jesus' youth, is venerated in St. Joseph's church.

The Jordan River
Where Jesus Was Baptised

The Jordan River is a major water source in this region that flows through the Jordan Rift Valley into the Dead Sea. It extends from tributaries at the base of Mount Hermon to its main source, the Kinneret, and then down to the Dead Sea. At a mere 250 kilometres, it is diminutive compared to other rivers around the world, but nevertheless has significant status in the many dry areas of Israel and Jordan, and for much of its route traces the political boundaries of Israel and Jordan in a north-south line.

The river is modest, and from some perspectives is little more than a stream or a creek. Near its headwaters, it meanders gently through small towns and fields, predominantly in the greener hills and valleys to the north. As it makes its way to the more parched lowlands to the south and toward the Dead Sea, it becomes depleted, struggling through the dry terrain.

Its significance extends into the Old Testament, where it is occasionally referenced. Its cultural identity in modern times is partly linked to its place in Judaism and Christianity, and in particular its significance in the baptism of Jesus. Christian pilgrims today visit the traditional site of Jesus' baptism at a place called

Yardenit, at the point where the Jordan River flows out of the Kinneret. John (The Baptist) and Jesus were relatives and had grown up together. John's mother, Elizabeth, had known from the beginning, even before Jesus was born, that her kinswoman Mary was going to be the mother of the Son of God, Jesus. It seems that John was not aware of Jesus' identity until this event at Jesus' baptism.

Jesus arrived from Galilee to John at the Jordan to be baptised by him. But John tried to make him change his mind. "I ought to be baptised by you", John said, and yet you have come to me!" But Jesus answered him, "Let it be so for now. For in this way we shall do all that God requires." So, John agreed.

As soon as Jesus was baptised, he came out of the water. Then the heaven was opened to him, and he saw the spirit of God coming down like a dove and lighting on him. Then a voice said from heaven, "This is my own dear Son, with whom I am pleased."

Jericho
The City of Palms

References to Jericho in the Old Testament are prolific. Reputed to be the one place on earth where civilisation traces back continuously for over 10,000 years, Jericho is located over 250 metres below sea level, circled by hills in a kind of natural amphitheatre and fed by underground springs. The works of God are abundantly referenced around Jericho, from mighty fire-and- brimstone battles to discoveries of spring waters that transformed agriculture in the region.

Jericho is the Biblical epicentre of the Israelites' return from bondage in Egypt, the first foothold to a promised land; a land of milk and honey. Unlike the fertile areas to the north of Israel, today Jericho is a dusty, almost barren place. Its streets are quiet and a thin film of yellow-orange dust coats almost everything. Shade is in short supply, as the town comprises scattered low buildings with the very occasional and startling medium-rise building breaking up the landscape.

In the New Testament, Jesus passed through Jericho. His parable of the Good Samaritan is set on the road between Jericho and Jerusalem.

The Mount of Temptation, immediately to the west of Jericho, is the location of Jesus' wanderings for 40 days and nights in the wilderness. Now accessible by a creaking, groaning cable car, the Mount offers panoramic views of the region. Despite its impressive, chronicled past, its historical presence is difficult to connect within its current, faded environment. In the Bible, Jesus healed blind Bartimaeus (Mark 10:46-52) and converted Zachaeus here (Luke 19:1-10).

When Jesus entered Jericho, Zacchaeus the wealthy chief tax collector wanted to see who Jesus was, but being a short man, he could not, because of the crowd. So, he ran ahead and climbed a sycamore fig tree to see him. When Jesus reached the spot, he looked up and said to him "Zacchaeus, come down immediately. I must stay at your house today." So, he came down at once and welcomed him gladly.

After His baptism by John, Jesus' fasted for 40 days and 40 nights in the Judean wilderness where the devil tempted Jesus, remembered now at a monastery on Quadrantal Mountain above Jericho and to the west of it. Although the devil offered him all kinds of splendours, Jesus refused to succumb to temptation. For this reason, the heights are also called the Mount of Temptation.

Then the Spirit led Jesus into the desert to be tempted by the Devil. After spending forty days and nights without food, Jesus was hungry. Then the devil came to him and said, "If you are God's son, order these stones to turn into bread." But Jesus answered, "The scripture says, *"Human beings cannot live on bread alone, but need every word that God speaks."*

Cana

The Place of Jesus' First Miracle

The town of Cana, due east of Nazareth and a short distance in today's terms from the Sea of Galilee, is a sleepy, undulating town with cobbled streets and older houses away from the main thoroughfare. It is credited with the first of Jesus' miracles, in which he turned water into wine during a wedding ceremony, when the groom's stock of wine had run out. Although seemingly trivial, the event marks a very important milestone in Jesus' life – that of his first publicly recognised miracle as the Son of God.

Today, winemakers flourish from the tourist trade; the shops overflow with visitors eager to buy a bottle of Cana wine, much of which is sweet and fortified. A winding lane leads to a church dedicated to Jesus' first miracle, which popularly serves as a wedding venue.

There was a wedding in the town of Cana in Galilee. Jesus' mother was there, and Jesus and his disciples had also been invited to the wedding. When the wine had run out, Jesus' mother said to him "They are out of wine."

"You must not tell me what to do," Jesus replied. "My time has not yet come." Jesus' mother then told the servants, "Do whatever he tells you." The Jews have rules for ritual washing, and for this purpose six stone water jars were there, each one large enough to hold between twenty and thirty gallons. Jesus said to the servants, "Fill these jars with water." They filled them to the brim, and then he told them, "Now draw some water out and take it to the man in charge of the feast." They took him the water, which now had turned into wine, and he tasted it.

He did not know where this wine had come from; so, he called the bridegroom and said to him, "Everyone else serves the best wine first, and after the guests have drunk a lot, he serves the ordinary wine. But you have kept the best wine until now!"

This miracle also reveals Christ's acceptance of St. Mary's intercession on the behalf of humans. For Christ Himself proclaimed to her saying "My hour has not yet come." However, because of his mother's plea, He immediately answered and performed the miracle.

Capernaum
The Town of Jesus

Capernaum was Jesus' second home, following his departure from Nazareth at the age of 30. It is on the northern shore of the Sea of Galilee, and by ancient standards is a well-connected town to places such as Damascus and to the central and southern parts of Israel. Today it seems forlorn and lost, retaining a quaint air of Biblical obscurity. Still, it is a momentous little town, as Jesus drew his first disciples from it, and began his teachings in earnest in the synagogue there. At first its modesty is a contradiction, as it does not seem a logical choice for the Son of God to proclaim a greater truth to all mankind. Yet it speaks to Jesus' humanity, of his first tentative steps to spread the word of this Father after his inglorious departure from Nazareth, and of his recruitment of faithful followers at a humble scale. It reflects his stance, not as a fierce heroic general in a battle against evil, but as a quiet and gentle messenger of peace.

The synagogue of Capernaum is impressive in size. Now all but obscured by centuries of damage, its courtyard and columns remain. The ruins of are saturated with Biblical carvings; old, blackened stones, some still actively studied by scholars and historians for more clues to the past.

As Jesus walked along the shore of Lake Galilee, he saw two brothers who were fishermen, Simon (called Peter) and his brother Andrew, catching fish in the lake with the nets. Jesus said to them, "Come with me, and I will teach you to catch people."

At once they left their nets and went with him.

Jesus went on and saw two other brothers, James and John, the sons of Zebedee. They were in their boat with their father Zebedee, getting their nets ready. Jesus called them and at once they left the boat and their father and went with him.

Peter, Andrew, James, and John were living in the village. Matthew the tax collector also dwelt here. Jesus told Mathew: "Come follow me." He left everything and followed Jesus.

Jesus went to the synagogue and began to teach. The people who heard him were amazed at the way he taught, for he wasn't like the teachers of the law; instead, he taught with authority.

Just then a man came into the synagogue and screamed, "What do you want with us Jesus of Nazareth? Are you here to destroy us? I know who you are – you are God's Holy messenger!"

Jesus ordered the spirit, "Be quiet, and come out of the man!" The evil spirit shook the man hard, gave a loud scream, and came out of him.

The people were all so amazed that they started saying to one another, "What is this? This man has authority to give orders to the evil spirits, and they obey him!"

The inhabitants of Capernaum often heard Jesus preaching and they witnessed more of his miracles than other people. They enjoyed listening to Jesus and flocked to him by the thousands. However, according to the Bible, they failed to repent and turn from all their words, behaviour and deeds.

Today the ruins are owned by two churches: the Franciscans control the western portion with the synagogue and the Greek Orthodoxy's property is marked by the white church with red domes.

Excavations had revealed one residence that stood out from the others. This house was the object of early Christian attention with 2nd century graffiti and a 4th century house church built above it. In the 5th century a large octagonal Byzantine church was erected above this, complete with a baptistery. Pilgrims referred to this as the house of the apostle Peter.

The Sea of Galilee
and Its Surroundings

Galilee is a resort area, renowned for its cooler, soothing climate, and its picturesque countryside. The Sea of Galilee is a freshwater lake, the lowest of its kind in the world, located below sea level. Fed by the upper Jordan River and exiting via the lower Jordan River, the Sea of Galilee is a focal point of water for north Israel.

Its shores are idyllic, and it is not difficult to picture a divine man preaching in and around the small fishing towns in ancient times. Permanent residents and visitors surround the lake, and it is readily navigable. Small fishing and commercial boats criss-cross its diameters from one shore to another, but boat traffic appears relatively sparse and unhurried. Although generally calm, it is big enough to create large waves in storms. The Sea is small, personal, and accessible; both sunrises and sunsets over water can be seen in one day.

Today, the Sea of Galilee is a major stopping point for tourists and pilgrims and is well serviced by comfortable inns and hotels. It is a place that entices people to stay a while, with its air of a quiet seaside resort. From the centre of this sea, it is possible to see many of the places referenced in the Bible. The relative solitude offered from the centre makes it an ideal place to reflect on the birthplace of new doctrine. In the mornings and evenings, boats take pilgrims out on the open water to offer their individual prayers, conduct small communal masses or bask in the pages of a two-thousand-year history.

The Sea of Galilee, known to Israelis as Lake Kinneret, is only 13 miles by 7 miles. It was on these beautiful shores that Jesus delivered sermons and performed miracles. Many famous sites are located around the lake, including Capernaum, home to at least five of the twelve disciples. It was here that Jesus met Simon Peter, James, and John, His first disciples, and it was here that He performed many miracles.

The pilgrims can take a boat trip leaving from Nof Ginnausor, where Jesus' boat was found and restored. They are then able to visit the Goalen heights, and Banais where Jesus told Peter *"On this rock I will build my Church."* Closer to the town of Jesus is **Tagbha**, a site that commemorates the Multiplication of the Loaves and Fishes by Jesus. When Jesus heard the news about John (the Baptist), he left there in a boat and went to a lonely place by himself. The people heard about it, and so they left their towns and followed him by land. Jesus got out of the boat, and when he saw the large crowd, his heart was filled with pity for them, and he healed their sick.

That evening his disciples came to him and said, "It is already very late, and this is a lonely place. Send the people away and let them go to the villages to buy food for themselves."

"They don't have to leave," answered Jesus. "You yourselves give them something to eat!" "All we have are five loaves and two fish," they replied.

Then bring them here to me," Jesus said. He ordered the people to sit down on the grass; then he took the five loaves and the two fish, looked up to heaven, and gave thanks to God. He broke the loaves and gave them to the disciples, and the disciples gave them to the people. Everyone ate and had enough. Then the disciples took up twelve baskets full of what was left over. The number of men who ate was about five thousand, not counting the women and children.

The mosaic of the fish and loaves is laid next to a large rock, which has caused some New Testament scholars to speculate that the builders of the original church believed that Jesus stood on this rock when he blessed the fish and loaves just before the feeding of the crowd who had come to hear him. The Church of the Multiplication of the Loaves and Fishes is also known as the Church of the Multiplication. The church is modern but stands on the site of 4th and 5th-century churches. It preserves a splendid early Christian mosaic as well as the traditional stone on which the miraculous meal was laid.

Matthew (5:3-11) tells that Jesus saw the crowds and went up a hill, where he sat down. His disciples gathered around him, and he began to teach them, rendering into history the famous Sermon on the Mount, in which he recounted the Beatitudes. Today, this hill is topped by a Catholic chapel built in 1939 by the Franciscan Sisters with the support of the Italian ruler Mussolini. The building which was constructed by the noted architect Antonio Barluzzi is full of numerical symbolism. In front of the church, the symbols on the pavement represent Justice, Prudence, Fortitude, Charity, Faith, and

Temperance. Inside the church hangs the cloak from Pope Paul VI's visit in 1964.

West of the Sea of Galilee, Mt. Tabor sits at the eastern end of the Jezreel Valley. Buses are no longer permitted to drive to the top of Mount Tabor and the site is accessible only by walking or biking a winding narrow road on the north side. Walkers can use 4,300 steps built in the 4th century AD for Christian pilgrims.

Matthew (17:1-3) explained the significance of Mt Tabor as follows: Jesus took with him Peter and James and his brother John and led them up a high mountain, by themselves. And he was transfigured before them, and his face shone like the sun, and his clothes became dazzling white. Suddenly there appeared to them Moses and Elijah, talking with him.

Then Peter said to Jesus, "Lord, it is good for us to be here. If you wish, I will make three dwellings here, one for you, one for Moses and one for Elijah. While he was still speaking, suddenly a bright cloud overshadowed them, and from the cloud a voice said, "This is my son, the Beloved; with him I am well pleased; listen to him!

When the disciples heard this, they fell to the ground and were overcome by fear. But Jesus came and touched them saying, "Get up and do not be afraid." And when they looked up, they saw no one except Jesus himself alone.

Dedication to suffering produces transfiguration and lets the glory of God shine forth. The Tabor experience was to strengthen Jesus - the end of His path of sorrows would also be supreme Glory.

Jerusalem
Where Jesus Was Crucified

Jerusalem is the site of one of the oldest cities on earth, with the beginnings of civilisation there dating back 6 millennia. The old city of Jerusalem dates back to a thousand years before the birth of Christ, when it was founded as the political capital of the ancient Kingdom of Israel, and then the Kingdom of Judah.

Jerusalem has been the epicentre of many historical battles, including modern day conflicts in the Middle East, and carries the dubious honour of being the site of the longest running conflicts in the history of humanity. It is a centre of religion, venerated by the Judaism, the modern-day Christian community, and the Islamic community. Famous for the Crusaders' savage occupation in the name of Jesus and England, and the Moslem General Saladin's subsequent victory to reclaim it for Islam, it has nevertheless enjoyed centuries of relative peace under Arab and Turkish rule.

This religiously themed history oozes out of the old city of Jerusalem, a walled city set above valleys, with a commanding position that made it a defensible fort and consequently the site of long, bitter, and savage battles. Dark, aromatic souks wind their way through the old city like cobbled snakes, the stone walls bearing the marks of centuries of use and renewal. Synagogues, mosques, and churches of many dominions are located within stones' throws of each other. Moslems and Jews know where the churches are; they even know where the Stations of the Cross are located. Christians know where the holy places of the Moslems and Jews are hidden. It is a city where the practitioners of the various religious beliefs seem to know about the other beliefs, often in astonishing detail. Yet it is not a city that lives in tolerance of other beliefs; there is a sense of tension that seems to emanate from the very foundations of the rock itself. Religious sites seem to compete for positioning in the landscape.

Visual imagery of Jesus' days still abounds, despite the significant Arabic overtones of old Jerusalem today. Jerusalem is like a time capsule; a walk through its narrow streets is like a walk-through passage of the Bible. A messiah preaching to his flock, perhaps astride a donkey and surrounded by inquisitive children, would not seem out of place there in the 21st century.

The Western or **Wailing Wall**, one of Judaism's most venerated sites, plays host to thousands of pilgrims a day. Today, a checkpoint is in the alleyways between the souks and the Western Wall; Israeli guards with semi-automatic rifles check bags for weapons, and airport security measures in the form of x- ray machines and metal detector arches control the entrance to this holy site. It abuts the stunning Al Akhsa Mosque, which is controlled by other armed guards.

The old city of Jerusalem is studded with the sites of the **Stations of the Cross**, momentous events along Christ's trail of persecution that led to his crucifixion. Astonishingly ancient and venerated sites are clustered around the symbolic site of his crucifixion. Artefacts from centuries past lie in abundance within the halls of the churches that jostle for positioning around this most sacred of holy grounds, representing millennia of accumulated historical reverence to the God and the Son of God.

Jerusalem can be entered via several gates. The different gates and the places they lead to are given here.

1. **The Zion Gate**: leads directly to the Armenian and Jewish quarters.

2. **The Dung Gate**: leads directly to the Western Wall and the Southern Wall Archaeological Park.

3. **Gate of Mercy**: This gate, in the eastern Temple-Mount wall, may be the best-known of them all.

Also called the Golden Gate or the Eastern Gate, it has been blocked for centuries, and is said to be awaiting a miraculous opening when the Messiah comes and the dead are resurrected.

4. **Lion's Gate**: which leads to the Pools of Bethesda, the Via Dolorosa, and the markets.

5. **Herod's Gate**: leads to the Old City markets, is also called the Flowers Gate.

6. **Damascus Gate**: This most imposing of Jerusalem's gateways also faces north and is named for the grand city from which Jerusalem's rulers once came.

7. **The New Gate**: This is the only Old City entry way not part of the original design of the 16th-century walls. It was breached in the waning days of the Ottoman Empire to allow Christian pilgrims quicker access to their holy places within the ramparts.

8. **The Jaffa Gate**: This was the destination of Jewish and Christian pilgrims when they made their way to the Holy City. Legend has it that every conqueror of Jerusalem will walk through this gate.

Outside the imposing walls of old Jerusalem, the countryside is dotted with other Biblical sites, fading into a community segmented largely into Arab and Jewish areas. Jerusalem remains a contradiction that defines the human condition; a spiritual place that is testament to the spirit of faith and hope of humanity and the tense undercurrent of intolerance that exposes humanity's worst traits. It is this contradiction that makes it a unique place and one for which the term "do unto others as you would have them do unto you" has certain poignancy.

Mount of Olives

The Mount of Olives is the hill facing the old city of Jerusalem, on the eastern side of Kidron valley. Its name came from the olive trees that once grew on its hillside from ancient times. Jesus had many encounters on Mount of Olives, and the area has many Churches that glorify his acts in this part of Jerusalem. From the top of Mount of Olives one can admire the spectacular views of the walled old city of Jerusalem.

Pool of Bethesda

This is the pool where Jesus healed a paralytic on a Sabbath day and consequently angered the Jewish Authorities.

John 5:1-15 tells that Jesus was once at Jerusalem for a religious festival, and he came upon a pool with five porches. A large crowd of people were lying on the porches – the blind, the lame and the paralysed. A man was there who had been sick for thirty-eight years. Jesus saw him lying there, so he asked him "Do you want to get well?" The sick man answered, "Sir, I don't have anyone here to put me in the pool when the water is stirred up. While I am trying to get in, somebody else gets there first."

Jesus said to him, "Get up, pick up your mat, and walk." Immediately the man got well; he picked up his mat and started walking.

The day this happened was a Sabbath, so the Jewish Authorities told the man who had been healed, "This is Sabbath, and it is against our Law for you to carry the mat." He answered, "The man who made me well told me to pick up my mat and walk." They asked him, "Who is the man who told you to do this?" But the man who had been healed did not know who Jesus was, for there was a crowd in that place, and Jesus had slipped away. Afterward, Jesus found him in the temple and said, "Listen you are well now; so, stop sinning or something worse may happen to you." Then the man left and told the Jewish authorities that it was Jesus who had healed him.

Palm Sunday Road to Dominus Flevit (Church)

It was on this road that Jesus rode a donkey to the Temple Mount and was sacrificed on the Mount of Olives four days later. The view from this road, toward the Dome of the Rock and the Old City, is breathtaking. The road is very steep and narrow and ends with the Tomb of the Virgin

Mary on the right and the Church of All Nations on the left.

Passion Sunday is also Palm Sunday. On Palm Sunday Christians celebrate the triumphal entry of Jesus Christ into Jerusalem, the week before his death and resurrection.

Matthew 21:1-11 tells us that as Jesus and his disciples approached Jerusalem, they came to Bethphage at the Mount of Olives. There Jesus sent two of the disciples on ahead with these instructions: "Go to the village there ahead of you and at once you will find a donkey tied up with her colt beside her. Untie them and bring them to me. And if anyone says anything, tell him, "The Master needs them"; and he will let them go at once. So, the disciples went and did what Jesus had told them to do. They brought the donkey and the colt, threw their cloaks over them and Jesus got on. A large crowd of people spread their cloaks on the road while others cut branches from the trees and spread them on the road. The crowds walking in front of Jesus and those walking behind began to shout, "Praise to David's Son! God bless him who comes in the name of the Lord! Praise be to God!"

When Jesus entered Jerusalem, the whole city was thrown into an uproar. "Who is he?" the people asked. "This is the prophet Jesus, from Nazareth in Galilee," the crowds answered. Dominus Flevit is the place where Jesus wept over the city of Jerusalem. A church was built here to mark this.

The Upper Room

The chief priests and the elders were planning secretly to arrest Jesus and put him to death. It was now the Passover festival time and they were hesitating to arrest him at this time as they thought the people would riot. They were looking for an opportune time, which was fast approaching – a time when Judas Iscariot was willing to betray him for thirty pieces of silver.

Jesus sent Peter and John to follow a man carrying a jar of water who was to show a large furnished room upstairs where they were to get everything ready for supper. The upper room is where Jesus instituted the Eucharist during the Last Supper, and where he washed the apostles' feet.

The Garden of Gethsemane

It would be nice to think that the olive trees in the Garden of Gethsemane could have been young saplings when Jesus came here with the disciples on that fateful night after the Last Supper; but of course, that was many centuries ago and the olive trees today are but distant descendants, or perhaps entirely re-planted trees. Still, the garden is reminiscent of the pivotal sections in the Bible where Jesus prayed to his father and agonised over the events to come.

In Matthew 26:36-39, we are told that Jesus went with his disciples to Garden of Gethsemane, and he said to them, "Sit here while I go over there and pray." He took with him Peter and the two sons of Zebedee. Grief and anguish came over him, and he said to them, "The sorrow in my heart is so great that it almost crushes me. Stay here and keep watch with me."

He went a little farther on, threw himself face downward on the ground, and prayed, "My father, if it is possible, take this cup of suffering from me! Yet not what I want, but what you want."

During the events that unfolded, leading up to his crucifixion, Jesus predicted that Peter would deny knowledge of him three times, a claim Peter vehemently rejected. Yet we are told in the Bible that Peter, Jesus' favourite disciple, did indeed deny knowing him when questioned on three separate occasions after Jesus' arrest. The Church of St Peter was erected in 1931 to commemorate Peter's triple rejection of Jesus and his subsequent remorse. It was built over the High Priest Caiphas' house. The extraordinary church interior is a giant, multi-coloured mosaic portraying New Testament figures.

Nearby, the Antonia Fortress was a military barracks built by Herod the Great in Jerusalem and named after Herod's patron Mark Antony. The fortress was built at the eastern end of the great wall of the city (the second wall), on the north-eastern side of the city, near the temple and Pool of Bethesda.

Traditionally, it has been thought that the vicinity of the Antonia Fortress later became the site of the Praetorium, and that this building was the place where Jesus was taken to stand before Pilate. The trial of Jesus before the Jewish Council (or **Sanhedrin**), following his arrest and prior to his trial before Pontius Pilate is called the Sanhedrin Trial of Jesus.

The Church of the Flagellation is a Roman Catholic Church located in the eastern section of Jerusalem, near the Saint Stephen's Gate. According to tradition the church enshrines the spot where Jesus Christ was flogged by Roman soldiers before his journey down the Via Dolorosa to Calvary. Also included in this complex are the Franciscan Monastery of the Flagellation, and the Church of the Condemnation and Imposition of the Cross.

The impressive Church of All Nations, relates the events of this place in brilliantly detailed floor- to ceiling mosaics: Jesus praying alone (Mark 14:35-36); Judas' betrayal of Jesus (Matt. 26:48); and the cutting off of the ear of the High Priest's servant (Mark 14:47).

The Stations of the Cross – The Via Dolorosa

The path which Jesus took from the Sanhedrim to Calvary is known as the Way of Sorrows or **the Via Dolorosa**. The first station in this sad journey is the Tower Church of the Flagellation Church of All Nations 31 of Antonia. Jesus was made to carry the Cross across down the noisy, crowded, narrow streets of Jerusalem. The streets are marked by nine Stations of the Cross. There have been fourteen stations, with the remaining five stations (10 – 14) being inside the Church of the Holy Sepulchre. The route is believed to have started just inside the Lions' Gate (St. Stephen's Gate), at the Umariya Elementary School, near the location of the former Antonia Fortress, and made its way westward through the Old City to the Church of the Holy Sepulchre.

The first and second stations commemorate the events of Jesus' encounter with Pontius Pilate, while Stations three, seven, and nine represents the three falls of Jesus under the weight of the Cross. The fourth station depicts Jesus with his mother Mary. The fifth station refers to Simon of Cyrene taking Jesus' cross and carrying it for him. The sixth station depicts a piece of cloth, known as the Veil of Veronica, as having been supernaturally imprinted with Jesus' image after it was used to mop his brow. The Eighth station commemorates Jesus' encounter with pious women on his journey.

Each Friday, a Roman Catholic procession walks the Via Dolorosa route, starting out at the monastic complex by the first station; the procession is organised by the Franciscans of this monastery, who also led the procession.

The Calvary

The Church of the Holy Sepulchre is within the walled Old City of Jerusalem. The site is venerated by many Christians as Golgotha, (the Hill of Calvary), where the New Testament says that Jesus was crucified, and is said to also contain the place where Jesus was buried.

Two sites in Jerusalem lay claim to being the tomb of Christ. Standing on Calvary (where Jesus was crucified), the Church of the Holy Sepulchre is mostly believed by Catholics to be the place where Jesus was buried.

In 1884, British General Charles Gordon discovered a garden tomb one block from the Old City wall, contending this was where Jesus was buried. When Gordon noted a rock formation on a curious hillside, he found a rock-cut empty tomb nearby. Based on scripture, Gordon believed his discovery was the true burial place.

The Church of the Primacy of Peter in Tabgha is a modest Franciscan chapel that commemorates Jesus' reinstatement of Peter after a fish breakfast on the shore, after his resurrection. In John 21, we are told that Jesus appears to his disciples for the Church of the Holy Sepulchre Catholic crowds gather for a brief glimpse of the Tomb of Christ 33 third time after his resurrection on the shores of the Sea of Galilee. The night before, Peter and several other disciples had sailed out on the lake to fish but caught nothing. In the morning, a man appeared on the shore and called out to them to throw their net on the right side of the boat. Doing so, they caught so many fish they couldn't drag the net back into the boat. At this point Peter recognizes Jesus, and promptly jumps out of the boat to wade to shore to meet him. The other disciples follow in the boat, dragging the net behind them. When they land, Jesus had prepared a charcoal fire for the fish and provided bread, and they have breakfast together (John 21:9).

This is believed to have taken place on the mensa Christi, a large rock incorporated in the chapel. After breakfast, Jesus reinstated Peter (after his three-time denial of Jesus at the crucifixion) with the words "Feed my sheep" (John 21:15-19).

This is the event for which the modern church is named, which is interpreted by the Catholic Church to give the Pope (as the successor of Peter) authority over the worldwide Church. A round Chapel of the Ascension commemorates the resurrection of Christ.

The Chapel of the Ascension in Jerusalem today is a Christian and Muslim holy site from which Jesus ascended into heaven. In the Chapel is a stone imprinted with what some claim to be the very footprints of Jesus. Near the Ascension Chapel is the Pater Noster Chapel where the Lord's Prayer is displayed in tablets on the walls in many languages.

From a manger in Bethlehem to the rock from which he ascended into Heaven, Jesus left a permanent mark upon our world, a consciousness of peace and forgiveness, a legacy of Christianity and a closer connection with God for many of the billions of people on Earth. His footsteps, obscured by the dust and destruction of many centuries, nevertheless remain in the spirits of His followers.

The pilgrims to the Holy land would thank the Lord for His grace in allowing them the opportunity to trace Jesus' footsteps and become closer with Him in spirit.

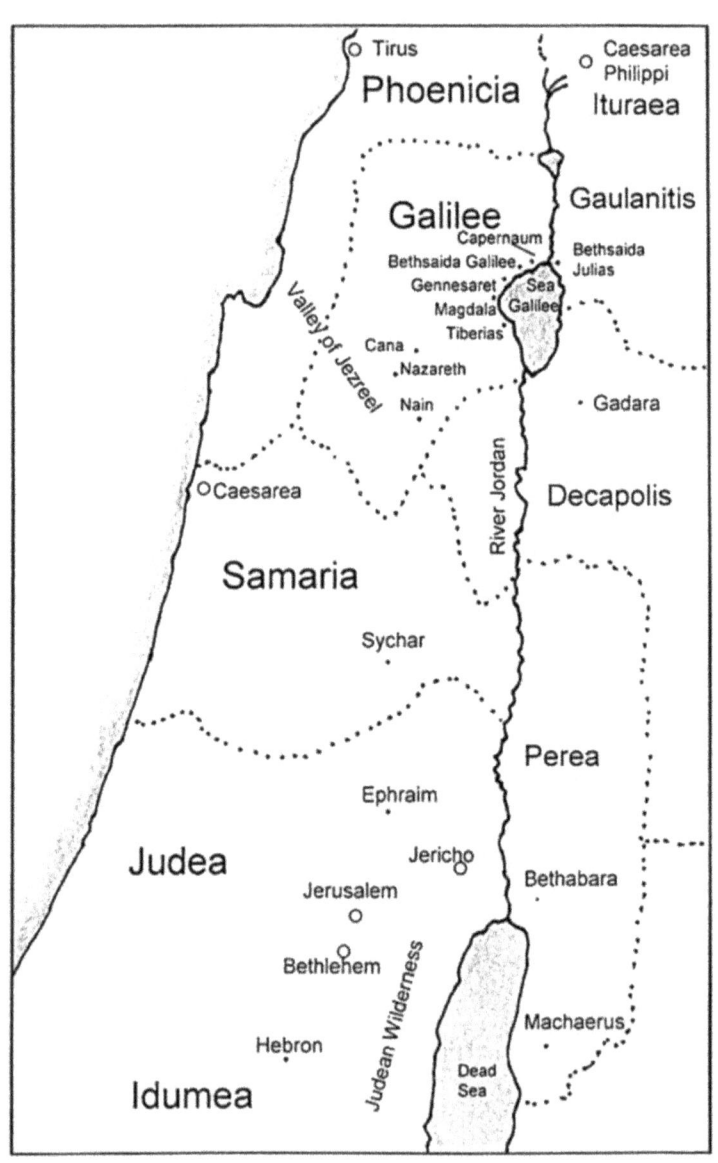

OUR MOTHER, MARY

Jesus' mother is also our mother

Catholics give respect to Mary and other Saints.

Jesus honoured Mary by changing water into wine at the Cana wedding. She was also told by Jesus on the cross, John would be her son.

Mary's miracles and apparitions are many.

CHAPTER 7
THE CATHOLIC CHURCH OF THE FUTURE

Every fervent Catholic child needs to grow up in the modern times with the following:

- Prayer habit
- Bible-knowledge
- Kindness
- The willingness to proclaim the Good News

Many people would agree that the Catholic Faith represents a complete system of ideas among all the competing philosophies of humanity.

Catholics living their faith are fully filled with light and joy. A devout catholic home has an atmosphere, a culture of goodness and holiness that is completely contagious. The sacraments Catholics receive are considered as precious gifts made available to them.

The greatest obstacle to the advance of evil in the world is seen as the Catholic Church. The Catholic Church which has been flourishing for more than twenty centuries is ever new. It is centered around a **true and living** God.

Jesus guarantees its **continued existence** despite persecutions, with Pope as her infallible head.

The Catholic Church proclaims that human life is sacred, and that the dignity of the human person is the foundation of a moral vision for society. Every person has an innate human dignity no one can take away. Human dignity is given freely to all human beings, whether saint or sinner, imprisoned or freed, powerful, or marginalised.

The Catholic Church teaches that all human life is sacred (sanctity of life) and that everyone has a right to life which should be protected and valued at every stage. The Catholic Church is against abortion in all circumstances. The Catholic Church teaches that life begins at conception.

A person is said to be fully initiated in the Catholic Church when they have received the three sacraments of Christian initiation namely, Baptism, Confirmation and Eucharist. This is achieved following a process of preparation.

Christianity began in Jerusalem and soon spread through the regions of Judea, Samaria, and neighbouring countries. Persecution from the Roman Empire drove away many believers. Centres of Christianity formed around the cities of Alexandria and Egypt, which became the roots for the Eastern Orthodox Church and Rome, which produced the Roman Catholic Church.

During its long history, the Catholic Church has been subject to criticism regarding her various beliefs and practices. Within the Church, this included differences of opinion regarding the use of Latin at Mass, and the subject of clerical celibacy (only unmarried men are ordained to priesthood).

More recent criticism focused on alleged scandals within the Church, particularly alleged financial corruption and the Catholic Church's sexual abuse scandals.

Pope Francis elected as the 266th Pope has made serious attempts at Catholic reform. Every effort is being taken to institute and implement dynamic changes suitable for the future.

He maintains the firm views of the Catholic Church regarding abortion (ending pregnancy) and Clerical celibacy

The celebration of the Eucharist in the Catholic Church has undergone significant changes over the years. These have been due to liturgical reforms and there is a fundamental shift in attitudes affecting the celebration of Eucharist today. This will change the way all Catholics think and worship in future years

What then are the possible changes expected in the Catholic Church of the future?

Pope benedict VI said that the Catholic Church would become a smaller but more faithful institution in the future. "It will be a Church that is more spiritual, poorer, and less political: a Church of the little ones."

Since 1970, weekly church attendance among Catholics has dropped, the number of priests declined and the number of people who have left Catholicism has increased.

Even with all the setbacks, Catholic religion is likely to be strong for at least another four decades according to some Catholic leaders. In the ensuing years anything can happen, but it is hoped that God will not allow the Church He himself instituted to suffer too much! In fact, one could expect the Catholic Church to begin to grow and be a world power.

Catholic population

Today, two thirds of the world's Catholics live in Africa, Asia, and Latin America.

Africa's Catholic population has grown exponentially in recent times. Almost three-quarters of the world's Catholics will live in Africa in the future. Assuming the current population trends continue, the largest Catholic national populations would be in Brazil, Mexico, the Philippines, the United States, the Congo, Uganda, Italy, Nigeria, and Argentina.

It is to be noted that 267 million Catholics in the year 1900 increased to 1.05 billion in 2000 and to 1.36 billion today (2022).

The global Catholic story is not one of steady decline but rather a rapid growth and this is expected to continue in the future.

Catholic Priests

In the years since World War II there has been a substantial reduction in the number of priests per capita in the Catholic Church.

The Catholic Church is facing difficult times because the number of people who are joining the clergy is less and therefore the talent pool is less than it was. Thus, the future of the Church looks very bleak, and it requires extraordinary faith.

In recent times, the number of priests in North America and Europe continued to decline but Africa and Asia saw a significant increase.

Clericalism

In practice, the clergy demand to be treated superior to the laity as they only decide about Church matters and other issues that impact the faithful in many aspects of their lives.

In the future it is likely that the Church, clerics, and the laity all will do their part in finding strategies for the good of the Church - the clerics, and for everyone.

Catholic worship methods

In order for Catholic faith to reach the hearts and minds of the laity, the Gospel needs to be presented in a way to which people can relate. This involves a process of expressing the life of the Church in local customs and habits of thought. The process is called inculturation.

The Church of Our Lady of Guadalupe (Mexico) is an extraordinary and wonderful example of inculturation.

A Catholic is basically required to live a Christian life, pray daily, participate in the sacraments, obey the moral laws, and accept the teachings of Christ and his Church. The minimum requirements for Catholics are attending Mass every Sunday and on Holy Days of Obligation and be good Catholics.

While watching Mass on TV, someone can reflect upon the readings, hear the homily, and pray along with the community at that Mass. These are all good and pious things that bring spiritual benefit. However, that benefit is not the same as a person, who is able to, being present in church with the Lord and receiving him in Communion.

The following suggested prayer could be recited during Communion time to receive Jesus spiritually.

PRAYER

I love you Jesus above all things, and
I desire earnestly to receive you into my soul.
Since I cannot at this moment receive you sacramentally,
come spiritually into my heart. Amen.

Exodus of Catholics to other faiths

The main reason for people leaving Catholicism is due to their inability to understand the Catholic Church's religious or moral beliefs and the reasons for Her stringent rules.

In order to be a true Catholic, one must truly believe that the Church was founded by Jesus and guided by the Holy Spirit. If there are any unclear dogmas or doctrines, they would eventually become clearer as one matures in age and wisdom. A Catholic must believe that they are under the right guidance of the Church, and that they are growing ever closer to the perfection of the kingdom of God.

The rate of growth of the Catholic Church depends on how soon every member of this unique institution becomes 'truly present' to one another in our local communities as well as in the global context in full union with our Lord and saviour Jesus Christ. When all people come to know Jesus and start following His teachings faithfully, **a Shining Life** would become a reality for each person.

www.ingramcontent.com/pod-product-compliance
Lightning Source LLC
LaVergne TN
LVHW050023080526
838202LV00069B/6897